Spi...
Into
Control

A Guide to Bringing
Balance Back
Into a Mother's Life

Dr. Sharon Phillips, Psy.D.

SPINNING
INTO
CONTROL

A Guide to Bringing Balance Back Into a Mother's Life

Dr. Sharon Phillips, Psy.D.

The views and opinions expressed in this work are those of the author and do not necessarily reflect the views and opinions of Braughler Books LLC.

Printed in the United States of America
First Printing, 2024

ISBN 979-8-89390-032-3

Library of Congress Control Number: 2024926346

Ordering Information: Special discounts are available on quantity purchases by bookstores, corporations, associations, and others. For details, contact the publisher at sales@braughlerbooks.com or at 937-58-BOOKS.

For questions or comments about this book,
please write to info@braughlerbooks.com.

Braughler™
Books
braughlerbooks.com

Dedication

To my mom, the original Superwoman.
I miss you more than words can say.

Table of Contents

Introduction

My Story

I am one of those people that have always kept a journal. My aunt gave me my first journal when I was in 4th grade, and over the years, I have kept quite a collection of journals--some only partially written in, others filled from cover to cover. Among many things, these journals help to serve as my memory, since a long-term memory is not one of my strengths!

One journal entry dated 8/31/99, when my first child was only four months old, is a prayer that reads in part:

"Dear Lord, I am confused about what You would have me to do with respect to my job...I ask You to help me in keeping a balance between being a mother and being a psychologist."

Nearly three years later and pregnant with my third child, I was still struggling with how to "do it all" as this entry dated 4/9/02 illustrates:

"Most heavenly Father, I come before you this morning with an ache in my heart from the night before that can only be described as an ache of longing for missing piece/peace. You are my missing piece and the peace that my soul is crying out for. I am failing at getting through my days alone. I am pregnant, weary, trying to accomplish a million things in just 24 hours, struggling not to lose my patience a hundred times a day, and learning, time

*after time again, what is truly important in life.
Nothing matters without You, Father. Life is hard,
and each moment is a battle sometimes, when the
babies are crying and teething and having one
temper tantrum after another, when I am just trying
to survive from naptime to bedtime, when the pager
is beeping and the calls of people from work are
beckoning, when one little person after another little
person demands my attention, my time, and my love,
and when Baby Michael kicks inside of me...."*

If that's not an accurate description of a woman out of
balance, I don't know what is! I praise God that I am in a
much different place today.

I am a living testimony to the challenge of balancing
the needs of work and family. Indeed, I have been right
there in the trenches side-by-side with you. My husband
and I had three sons in four years. I started this book when
they were young, and they are now all grown and living
on their own. They are 25, 23 and 22 years old. Although
I now work primarily with older adults in senior living
communities, for most of their school years, I worked about
40 hours a week in my own private practice as a clinical
psychologist, specializing in children and families. My
husband is an ordained minister, and his last full-time job
was working as a computer engineer. However, he has been
at home on disability and unable to work outside the home
since our youngest son was five years old due to recurrent
problems and chronic pain stemming from multiple failed
back surgeries and an incurable, degenerative disorder
known as arachnoiditis.

When our children were younger, we used a variety of daycare options for our three children, including daycare in another mother's home, babysitters who came to our home, and a Christian daycare center. During our last season needing childcare, my husband watched our children during the hours that I worked. As our children grew, I developed the principles that this book is based on and found that I was able to create a much better balance for myself between work and family. That's not to say that I didn't still have moments that were like those described in the despairing journal entries noted above. The difference is that those times were just that--moments--and not the status quo of my life. Overall, I was able to feel much more centered, peaceful, and balanced. That doesn't mean that I didn't still get stressed out at times, or that I didn't lose my temper at my kids on occasion, but what it does mean is that when those incidences occurred, I became much better at being able to get myself and my life back in balance without too much time going by.

I want all of this and more for you! If you are reading this book right now, chances are that you are struggling with this juggling act in your own life, and are looking for answers about how to "do all of this" better. As I mentioned before, I have been right there in the trenches with you. In my own search at how to "do all of this" better, I read many books and asked many people how they were able to:

- stay in close relationship with God,

- keep their households running smoothly,

- maintain a positive connection with their spouses,

- excel at work, school, and home,

- have quality and quantity time with
  their children,

- make time for themselves,

- develop and maintain healthy friendships, and

- make the best use of their volunteer time.

What I learned from my reading and from my conversations with other moms was extremely valuable and each contribution helped me to get one step closer to achieving this balance on my own. However, what was missing for me during my own struggle was a clear, step-by-step way to evaluate exactly where my life was out of balance, and what I specifically needed to do to turn things around. In essence, I had lots of pieces to the puzzle, but no template for how things could be best put together. I had a number of theories and important points to consider, but I lacked a more systematic approach on how to apply these ideas to my own life.

That's where the birth of this book came into being. It contains helpful quizzes and practical worksheets to help you as a mom apply the principles of balancing your life day-by-day. It is a "how-to" book. The basic premise of this book is that each person needs to evaluate her own individual "plates" of responsibilities in order to effectively balance her life. This book offers a number of different ways that this balance can be achieved for each area in a mother's life. You are encouraged to try any or all of the ideas in each chapter, in the hope that something mentioned on one of its pages will provide a good "fit" for you, and will help you keep that part of your life in balance with the others. If you are like me, you probably already have many ideas yourself to add to the ones mentioned in this book, and it would be wise for you to test out and experiment with those ideas as well in your search for balance in your life.

My prayer for you is that you will find among these pages a hope, a peace, and a joy that comes from living a life of harmony. May God be with you on this journey.

"And the peace of God, which transcends all understanding, will guard your hearts and your minds in Christ Jesus."
Philippians 4:7

Chapter 1

The Myth of
the Superwoman

We are all familiar with the "Superwoman" syndrome. It's the pressure every mother feels about being able to "do it all"--while smiling! It gives us no allowance for failure, no need for improvement, and no sympathy necessary from those around us. After all, Superwoman implies being super-human; she is the epitome of perfection. She doesn't need anything!

Who is this Superwoman, anyway? Let's take a look at her in all aspects of her life, so that we might become more familiar with her. Here is a description of what she looks like.

Superwoman fulfills all of her duties as a paid employee on her job perfectly. She meets all of her deadlines, reaches all of her goals, and is never late to work. All the phone calls she makes are job-related, her desk is organized and uncluttered, and her computer is always plugged into only work-related Internet sites. Superwoman is a stellar employee, who always achieves every promotion she desires, is remarkable at being a team player, and regularly shares in only character-building conversations in the breakroom. Who wouldn't want to have her in their company?

Within her immediate family, Superwoman meets all of their needs all of the time. She has daily romantic moments with her spouse, is always on time to pick up her children, and is never too tired to play with her kids. She volunteers regularly at her children's schools and has figured out how to manage the many hats she wears without feeling the least bit stressed. Superwoman has unending patience, never loses her cool, and manages the various challenges her children present with style and grace. Within her extended family, Superwoman helps care for her aging parents and is a devoted member of the "sandwich generation". She also has superb relationships with all of her siblings, and there is never any sibling rivalry or any amount of conflict between them.

Superwoman has a great social life! She has close female friends, a solid network of couples' friends that she shares with her husband, and regularly scheduled social events. Superwoman is a wonderful confidant, makes friends easily, and is the first one to bring over a covered dish for the new mother on the street. She is always comforting, never judgmental, and has never experienced jealousy over any of her friends' lives. After all, why would she? She's Superwoman!

Superwoman has a deep and close relationship with the Lord. Without fail, she rises early each morning to pray and to get into the Word. She always feels connected to God and is able to accept each trial He sends her way with nothing short of gratitude and praise. Superwoman has many scriptures memorized and is always able to recall them whenever she needs to. At her church, Superwoman is a devoted member of her congregation. She heads up several church ministries, always maintains the perfect balance of professionalism and warmth, and draws people closer to Christ on a regular basis. Even with all her church responsibilities, Superwoman never spreads herself too thin, and she has never been faced with conflicting demands between other people's needs and the needs of her family.

Superwoman keeps up with her household tasks without fail. Everything is in perfect order all the time, and her house always has that "just-cleaned" fragrance in it. She serves her family only homemade and nutritious meals, in proper proportion to the FDA's recommended food pyramid structure (or whatever the latest nutrition guidelines are!). The laundry in Superwoman's house is always freshly washed and neatly folded in their proper drawers. No one has ever had to weed through a pile of clean clothes in a laundry basket to find a pair of white socks to wear in the morning!

Financially, Superwoman is an example of perfection (what else would she be?). She balances her checkbook without error every month, never goes over budget on any item, and always pays her bills on time. She never has to ask herself the question of, "Should I pay the light bill this month or buy those new shoes my daughter needs for school?". Superwoman tithes without fail, is both thrifty and generous with her money, and has the appropriate amounts of cash saved away for emergencies, her children's future college needs, and her retirement (to the exact totals and percentages recommended by her financial advisor).

Superwoman is the ideal student. She is constantly focusing on continuing her education and is always enrolled in at least one class at a local college or university (since she wants to continually learn new things!). Her term papers are precisely written and tailored specifically to meet each teacher's exact expectations. She would never even think to tamper with the margins of her papers in order to have them reach the required page number limit! All her work is expertly proofread and there are never any typos or run-on sentences in her writing. Each and every piece of work is turned in on time and outside activities never interfere with the demands and requirements of her coursework. Superwoman actively participates in every class, is never absent, and always treats her fellow students with patience and kindness. She is the first to volunteer her notes to an absent student (since she never misses class!) and consistently offers to get her fellow classmates "up to speed" when they are struggling with the course material.

Oh, and did I mention Superwoman's physical appearance? Boy, does this woman have it together! Her hair is neatly styled; her makeup, flawless. She only wears clothes in the latest style and there is never a wrinkle or a hint of a stain on them. She would never go anywhere with spit-up on her shoulder or with a toddler's handprint on her leg. Her skin is without blemishes, and her eyes never look worn or tired (because of course, she gets the necessary eight hours of sleep each and every night!) Superwoman exercises regularly to maintain her girlish figure and takes time for herself frequently without fail. She has weekly appointments at the salon and gets manicures and massages on a frequent basis. Superwoman has both the time and the energy (of course!) to develop her individual hobbies and interests, including scrapbooking, gardening, and cooking.

If, after learning about Superwoman and her perfect life, you are feeling a little bit like plotting her demise, you are not alone! The above description may be tongue-in-cheek, but in essence, it reflects the struggle we all face at trying to do it all and be it all. As much as we might deny the existence of Superwoman in our own lives, there are elements of her that each of us as mothers strives to achieve, either on a conscious or on an unconscious level. Some of us may try to keep our homes looking immaculate (even with three children under the age of five underfoot daily!). Those of us who work outside the home may try to "bring home the bacon, fry it up in the pan", and then wash and dry all those greasy plates and silverware afterwards! Still others of us may find ourselves volunteering for every ministry at our church that invites our participation, believing that we are "indispensable" and that these activities surely could not be run as smoothly without us! No wonder we are burned out, stressed out, tired, and depressed. Perfection (i.e. Superwoman) DOES NOT EXIST! Or of it does, it is only for a "glimmer", an instance, before it disappears.

We can never be Superwoman. That's the bad news. The good news is that we can have our priorities in order and our "ducks in a row" if we would just learn another way of achieving balance, one that requires far less time and effort than trying to mimic Superwoman's ways.

Chapter 2

An Alternative Analogy: The Plate-Spinning Act

Instead of going down that impossible road of trying to achieve the perfection offered by Superwoman, I'd like to offer instead the analogy of the "plate-spinning" act.

Remember that circus act where the person enters onto the stage with a series of plates that are then set into motion one-by-one? There is a moment (and not longer than a moment) when, after each plate has been spun once, all the plates continue spinning in the air simultaneously and the person stands back while the audience claps in awe. What an incredible feat! However, immediately after this brief interlude, in order to keep all the plates spinning in the air at the same time, the person in charge of this act must go back to the first plate and begin spinning it again, and then go down the line to the next plate, and then the next plate, in order to keep them from all crashing down together.

This is the reality of how our lives are. It is IMPOSSIBLE to keep all our plates spinning at the same time for very long. There may be moments when this happens, but they are exactly that: moments. More realistically, what happens in our daily lives is that we have several things in our life running smoothly, at the same time that several other things in our life are in need of our attention. We must develop a habit of continually assessing:

a.   **which "plate"** in our busy lives requires our attention

b.   at **which time,** and then decide

c.   **which strategies** we need to implement to get this area of our life back on track.

Let's look for a moment at what each of these plates in the plate-spinning act represents. I believe that there are eight primary plates in every mother's life:

Figure 1 : 8 Primary Plates

| Plate 1: Religious/ Spiritual | Plate 2: Family | Plate 3: Job/Career | Plate 4: Education/ School |
| Plate 5: Household Tasks | Plate 6: Friendships/ Social Life | Plate 7: Self | Plate 8: Volunteer Activities |

Plate 1) Religious/spiritual: This plate encompasses all your responsibilities and commitments related to religion (e.g. being a member of a specific church) as well as those related to your own individual relationship with God (e.g. prayer time, Bible study, meditation). It includes any ministries that you are involved in at your church as well as the time that you spend relating to God outside of church.

Plate 2) Family: This includes your immediate family (e.g. spouse/partner, children) as well as any other individuals living with you in your home (e.g. aging parents, foster children, grandparents, grandchildren, nieces/nephews). It also includes your own parents, grandparents, siblings, and all other members of your extended family not otherwise listed.

The activities included on this plate pertain to all the responsibilities related to your family, including driving children to and from activities, attending sports events, enjoying "date nights" with your spouse or partner, and playing with your kids.

Plate 3) Job/Career: This is defined as any paid employment that you have, including part-time and full-time work positions. This plate can be made up of a home-based business, a consultant-type position, a small business you own yourself, or a more traditional employer-employee relationship for an outside corporation or agency. If you watch other children in your home for a fee, own your own business, or work for someone else, the time you devote to those responsibilities are reflected on this plate. Also included is the time you spend commuting back and forth to your job and any work that you do from your home (such as bringing home office paperwork).

Plate 4) Education/School: This category is made up of any outside coursework, classes, or workshops that you may attend. You may be working towards completion of a degree-oriented program, taking one or two courses of interest at your local community college, fulfilling continuing education classes in your chosen career field, or learning a new skill or trade. All of the time and energy you devote to these activities are reflected on this plate.

Plate 5) Household Tasks: This plate represents all the time and activities that are involved in the care and maintenance of your home. It includes chores like dishes, dusting, mopping floors, vacuuming and laundry; tasks such as shopping for, preparing, and serving meals; and other responsibilities like washing the car and mowing the grass. It involves the time you spend making appointments to get the air conditioning fixed, waiting for the person to hook up your cable t.v., and surfing the Internet to find the best deal on the new tile for your kitchen floor. The time and energy you spend creating and carrying out a budget, paying bills, and avoiding calls from telemarketers (!) also fall on this plate.

Plate 6: Friendships/Social Life: This plate includes all of your friendships and the time and responsibilities that come with being a friend. It includes friendships with other women, friendships you and your husband have with other couples, and friendships where your entire family socializes with another family. It may include evenings out, parties, or entertaining at your home. It also includes tasks like sending Christmas cards, remembering and celebrating birthdays, and watching another mom's children for a couple of hours while she runs some errands.

Plate 7) Self: This plate includes the time you spend on the activities you do for yourself. It may include hobbies such as scrapbooking or stamping, musical instruments such as playing the guitar, or ways you like to spend your leisure time such as exercising, doing crossword puzzles, or gardening. It also involves the time you spend doing your hair or make-up each day, as well as the time you spend getting your hair cut, your nails done, or your eyebrows waxed!

Plate 8) Volunteer Activities: Included on this plate are all the things you do for your children's schools (such as helping out with fundraising or spending time in your child's classroom), for your neighborhood (such as organizing block parties or taking meals to a sick neighbor), and for the community at large (such as participating in a club for moms, being a member of your local Chamber of Commerce, or taking part in a Woman's League).

Keep in mind that the plates listed above are not always as separate as they appear to be in the diagram. In reality, many activities can be included on more than one plate (such as a church activity that includes the plates of Religious/Spiritual, Family, Volunteer Activities, and Social Life). Remember learning about Venn diagrams in elementary school? These are diagrams where circles overlap and in this case, where your life plates overlap with one another. For example, being your child's soccer coach may include Family, Volunteer, Self (if you also love soccer), and maybe even Friendships/Social Life (Figure 2).

Figure 2 : Overlapping Plates

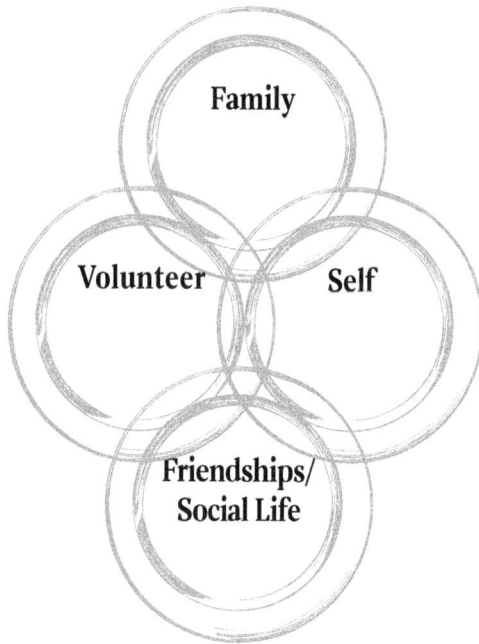

Exercise 1 – Identifying and Understanding the Plates in Your Life:

Now that you have read the general description of what each plate represents, take a few minutes to identify a specific description for what each plate represents in your own life. For each task and activity that you list, even though it may fall onto more than one plate, pick the plate that it best represents and list it there.

To help you with categorizing your activities onto various plates, below is an outline of common activities that pertain to each particular plate. Complete the outline so that it reflects your individual life.

Plate 1) Religious/spiritual:

- Worship at religious services.
- Meditation/quiet time/personal devotions.
- Prayer.
- Listening to religious music.
- Reading religious/spiritual books.
- Participating in or leading ministries at church.
- Family devotions time.
- Cards/phone calls to bereaved or sick and shut-in church members.
- Bible study.
- Small group activities.
- Other: _____
- Other: _____
- Other: _____

Plate 2) Family:

- Spending time with spouse/significant other.
- Spending time with children.
- Driving kids to and from activities.
- Scheduling and attending appointments and events with children or spouse/partner, such as doctor visits, dental visits, and ice cream socials.
- Caring for aging parents.
- Keeping in touch with your in-laws.
- Calling, visiting, or writing/e-mailing to parents, siblings, other relatives.
- Time spent caring for/being with pets.
- Other: _____
- Other: _____
- Other: _____

Plate 3) Job/Career:

- Time spent commuting to/from work.
- Time spent at work.
- Doing work that has been brought home.
- Work-related phone calls.
- Behind-the-scenes preparation for work tasks.
- Public speaking.
- Attending networking events.
- Surfing the Internet for work-related information.
- Marketing your business.
- Other: _____
- Other: _____
- Other: _____

Plate 4) Education/School:

- Getting information about courses/registering for classes/purchasing necessary books and supplies.
- Attending classes/workshops/seminars.
- Writing or reading required for individual assignments.
- Meeting with other class members to work on group assignments.
- Researching topics on the Internet or at the library.
- Other: _____
- Other: _____
- Other: _____

Plate 5) Household Tasks:

- Chores involved in taking care of your home, such as vacuuming, dusting, making the beds, taking out the garbage and cleaning bathrooms.

- Duties of feeding your family, including grocery shopping, planning and preparing meals, ordering pizza, going through the fast food drive-thru and doing the dishes.

- Jobs involved with clothing your family, including shopping for clothes, visiting the dry cleaners, sorting/washing/drying/folding clothes, deciphering what on earth would have made that magenta- colored stain, mending necessary items, and putting laundry away.

- Financial responsibilities, such as creating and following a budget, paying bills, going to the bank, purchasing stamps at the post office, and balancing your checkbook on Quickbooks (for those of us disciplined enough to do this!).

- Taking care of your cars, including washing them, arranging for necessary repairs, vacuuming out the stray French fries from behind the back seats, and wiping off little fingerprints and nose prints from the car windows.

- Other: _____

- Other: _____

- Other: _____

Plate 6) Friendships/Social Life:

- Keeping in touch with friends, whether it be via e-mail, phone calls, letters, or Christmas cards.

- Getting together with friends for lunch, playdates with your kids, or a monthly "Girls' Night Out".

- Chatting with your neighbor over the backyard fence.

- Planning, hosting, or attending celebrations for special events.

- Socializing with your husband and other couples.

- Preparing a meal for a family with a new baby in their home.

- Other: _____
- Other: _____
- Other: _____

Plate 7) Self:

- Pursuing activities of interest to you (e.g. scrapbooking, playing the piano, journaling, or gardening).
- Time and energy spent exercising (e.g. on the treadmill at the gym, lifting weights in your basement or walking in your neighborhood).
- "Beauty-based" activities such as going to the salon, having your hair highlighted, treating yourself to a manicure or pedicure, or shopping for new make-up.
- Relaxing activities, including taking a hot bath, reading a magazine, sitting in the sunshine or taking a much-needed nap!
- Other: _____
- Other: _____
- Other: _____

Plate 8) Volunteer Activities:

- Spending time at your child's school and participating in an activity there, such as planning the annual carnival, counting collected box tops, or reading to a child in the hall.
- Focusing on assisting those less fortunate than you by doing things such as bringing a meal to a sick and shut-in neighbor, serving in a soup kitchen, or preparing dinner for your local Ronald McDonald's House.

- Activities focused on your immediate neighborhood, such as helping plan your neighborhood's block party, organizing a petition to have streetlights installed in your subdivision or starting a babysitting co-op.
- Other: _____
- Other: _____
- Other: _____

Exercise 2 – Evaluating Your Plates

Now that you have spent some time reflecting and reviewing on which plate each task and responsibility of yours should fall, take a deep breath and pat yourself on the back for all the things you are now aware of that you do! Insulate yourself from becoming overwhelmed by reflecting on the scripture reference, "With God, all things are possible" (Matthew 19:26).

Let's take a moment to identify three plates in your life today, RIGHT NOW!, which (by the grace of God, perhaps!) are going rather smoothly. List those three plates below:

1.

2.

3.

In the same way, now take a moment to reflect on your life and write down no more than three plates that you feel could benefit from your increased time, attention, and solution-oriented strategies:

1.

2.

3.

Make a habit of doing this on a weekly basis, or whenever you are starting to feel burned out, stressed out, tired, or depressed about balancing the many responsibilities in your life. Once you have these two categories of plates in perspective (i.e. those that are "spinning well", and those that need to be "spun some more"), you will be able to pinpoint which plates you need to direct your attention to more specifically, and which plates you can leave alone for the time being. Each subsequent chapter in this book will focus on one plate at a time, and will have suggestions, ideas, tips, solutions, and tried-and-true techniques from other moms JUST LIKE YOU to help you get your life back in balance. Hang in there....and keep reading!!

Chapter 3

Staying in Close Relationship with God

Plate 1: Religion/Spirituality

By far, the most challenging plate for me to keep in balance on a regular basis is Religion/Spirituality. This might come as a surprise to you, because don't I, as a Christian woman, (and the wife of an ordained minister, no less!) have this one under control? The answer is a resounding, "NO!". Before I attempt to explain my struggle in this area, let me clarify the distinction I make between "religion" and "spirituality".

To me, "religion" refers to the man-made, public declaration of formal tenets or beliefs that is organized within a particular denomination (or a specific non-denomination). Among other things, religion defines the rituals practiced, the manner in which worship is celebrated in a particular church, and the various ministries that are organized within that church's community. In contrast, "spirituality" is based upon one's own personal relationship with God, and the way an individual relates to Him on a daily basis. I have met many people who have opposed organized religion because of its flaws and yet have a very close and intimate relationship with the Lord. In contrast, I also know several folks who are heavily into "religion" but lack a fundamental awareness of what a personal relationship with Jesus has to offer. To me, both are important. We are created to exist within a community and being involved and active in a community of other believers is an essential part of our Christian walk. However, we must also prioritize our own personal relationship with the Lord, for it is through individual prayer, reflection, praise, worship, and meditation on Scripture that we are guided by the Holy Spirit and directed towards God's purpose for our lives.

That said, let me get back to sharing with you my own difficulty with keeping Christ first in my life on a consistent basis, and why I believe this struggle exists.

First, I know that spiritual warfare does indeed exist. The enemy does not want me rooting my foundation firmly in the Lord, because then I have that much more time and energy freed up to waver from the Truth. In other words, as a soldier in the army of the Lord, I am only useful to God when I am fighting for Him. The enemy has a far lesser chance of winning me over to the side of darkness if my focus and intentions are solely on serving the Lord and carrying out His purpose for me.

Second, being a busy mom like you, I have hundreds of things vying for my attention at any given moment. "Do I get the breakfast dishes done or sit on the floor and play with my 2-year-old?" "Do I want to throw in an extra load of laundry in the washer, work out on the treadmill, or just sit passively in front of the TV?" "Do I spend my children's naptime calling a friend and catching up, surfing the Internet, or reading the Bible?" I know you know what I'm saying, because I know that you, too, are asking yourself these same questions day in and day out. As Joanna Weaver noted in her book, "Having a Mary Heart in a Martha World" we can easily become consumed in the "tyranny of the urgents" and neglect the most important thing of all—the only thing that we bring into eternity—our souls. Is it any wonder, then, that folding some of the seemingly-unending piles of clean laundry vies for fierce competition with writing in a spiritual journal and reflecting on a particular scripture verse?

The third reason that I experience this struggle to keep God first in my life is that, just like with all the other plates, there is a proper balance and order that must be kept in order to achieve harmony. I cannot neglect my responsibilities as a wife and mother by letting my kids run wild in the streets and allowing the housework to fall by the wayside, while I snuggle up with my Bible and my highlighter for hours on end. At the same time, when I set out to accomplish all my "earthly" tasks first, leaving little (if any) time and energy left over for prayer and Scripture reading, I find my well running dry, my tank running empty, and my patience wearing thin.

You may ask yourself, when can I possibly find time to spend with God on a daily basis, when I have so many other things on my plate? Here are some suggestions for when you can schedule in this activity:

a. First thing in the morning (wake up before your household wakes up).

b. When your children are napping or otherwise occupied (perhaps with their favorite T.V. show).

c. When your husband is available and can relieve you for a while.

d. During lunchtime while you are at work or on the job.

e. Before retiring at night—after putting the kids to sleep.

In order to decide which time of day would work best for your individual needs, experiment with having your "quiet time" at different times of the day. Keep in mind that your "quiet time" might be held at different times, depending on your schedule for a particular day. It is good to have a "Plan A" preferred time of day, as well as "Plan B" and "Plan C" alternatives, for those days when "Plan A" does not work out. For example, my preferred time of day (i.e. my "Plan A") was always early in the morning, before my kids woke up. Sometimes, though, either I woke up late or my kids woke up early! In this case, my Plan B was lunchtime (whether I was at home that day or at work). I also had a Plan C, for those days when both Plan A and Plan B fall through—and that is at night, after my kids were in bed, but before I turned in for the night.

Once you do find an opportunity for your own "quiet time", the next question is how can you spend this time so that it draws you closer to God? Here is a partial list of some activities you can do during your daily "quiet time":

a. Read the Bible and meditate on a specific Scripture reference or passage.

b. Write in a spiritual journal. (For more information on keeping a spiritual journal, refer to the book by this title listed in the recommended reading list at the end of this chapter.)

c. Read a book by a Christian author. (See list of recommended reading at the end of this chapter.)

d. Conduct an individually structured Bible study following a workbook, such as one of Beth Moore's or Max Lucado's workbooks. (Again, refer to the list of resources at the end of this chapter.)

e. Listen to praise or worship music.

f. Sit in silence and wait to hear what God wants to reveal to you. (Refer to "Discerning the Voice of God" by Priscilla Shirer.)

g. Pray about guidance in today's and tomorrow's "to-do" list and ask for God's assistance in determining which obligations need to take priority and which ones are of less importance.

Even with all these ideas, you might still wonder what quiet time could look like. Let me give you a peek into my own quiet time to share with you what works for me. (Keep in mind that this snapshot is one of how things went on an ideal morning, not one in which I overslept, or my kids—for whatever reason—were up before dawn!) In the morning, I woke to my alarm at 6:00 a.m., at which time the house was quiet and the sky was still dark. My husband would still be sleeping while I made my way downstairs. I started my coffeemaker and while waiting for the coffee to brew, I would go to the cabinet where I kept my books, and take out my Bible, my journal, and whatever spiritually filled book or workbook I was currently going through. I also kept a file box of scripture verses in the same cabinet, which included my personal concordance of words that referenced specific scriptures that had meaning to me. Sometimes I would pull this file box out as well. With my fresh cup of coffee in hand, I would then sit down at my dining room table, which has always been one of my favorite parts of the house, but a room that rarely gets used. (We tend to be more "kitchen/family room" people than "dining room" people, although I love the richness and formality of how the dining room feels.) I would arrange my coffee cup, my Bible, and my other materials in front of me, and bring a candle to the table to light, symbolizing my personal way of acknowledging the presence of the Lord during this time.

One of the first things I would always do is write in my journal. I might write a prayer to God thanking Him for specific blessings of which I am aware or asking Him for prayer requests for myself or those I care about. Sometimes I would jot down the events of the previous day so that I could mark them down for my memory or else I might record my plans for the day so that I could sort out what my day will look like. At other times, I simply wrote a poem expressing what was in my heart. After writing in my journal, I usually opened up my Bible as I also started going through the next chapter of the book I was reading or the next lesson of the workbook I was following. I kept an eye on the clock now and then, and when it was time, after blowing out the candle and placing my empty coffee cup in the sink, I headed back upstairs to start getting ready for the day, feeling emotionally refreshed and spiritually renewed (even if I might be still physically tired).

But don't take my word for it! If you are still uncertain whether religion/spirituality must come first in your life, with all the other responsibilities calling your name, I invite you to go through the following exercise to determine this unequivocally for yourself.

Exercise 3 – Understanding Why Your Spiritual Life Must Take Priority:

Step One: Conduct a personal experiment for a 2-week time frame. For one week during this time, set aside anywhere from 15-30 minutes per day that you agree to devote solely to time with God (this will be referred to as your "quiet time"). For the other week of this time, do not set aside any special quiet time with God, but instead focus your attention primarily on the other 7 plates in your life. You can choose which days you will have your "quiet time" and which days you will not devote "quiet time" with the Lord. For example, you might decide to specify "even-numbered days" for your "quiet-time days", and "odd-numbered days" for "non-quiet time days". Another option is to commit yourself to daily quiet time for the first seven consecutive days, and then not have any daily quiet time for the last seven consecutive days. Any way you decide to do this is fine.

Step Two: Keep a separate journal entry for each of these 14 days. For each of the 14 days, spend 5 minutes each day in recording the following:

1) Level of Stress Experienced Today:

Low---High

1	2	3	4	5	6	7	8	9	10

2) Amount of Patience Felt Today:

Low---High

1	2	3	4	5	6	7	8	9	10

3) Level of Inner Peace Experienced Today:

Low---High

1	2	3	4	5	6	7	8	9	10

4) Productivity Level Today (Ability to Accomplish Things):

Low---High

1	2	3	4	5	6	7	8	9	10

Step Three: Now do an analysis of your experience conducting this experiment by evaluating the entire two-week period and looking at each journal entry individually. Compare and contrast the difference in ratings on the days you chose to devote one-on-one time with the Lord, and the days you decided not to commit this one-on-one time. Are you convinced of the importance yet? If not, just continue the experiment for a longer time . . . I am certain you will see the results!

Chapter 4

Plate 2a: Maintaining a Positive Connection with Your Spouse

The best gift you can give your children is a happy marriage. This is a statement that I first heard years ago, and one I find myself repeating regularly to the families that I work with in therapy. Although it might first come as a surprise to you, I believe that with a little self-reflection and introspection, you will undoubtedly find this to be true. Think back to your own family of origin, and the relationship that was modeled to you by your parents of how a mother and a father should relate to each other. Do you recall an affectionate relationship between them, one that was characterized by a display of mutual respect and a genuine fondness for one another? Or do you remember two people who were disconnected from each other, perhaps finding themselves consumed primarily with work, child rearing, or their own personal struggles? Perhaps there was a high degree of marital conflict in your home growing up, and you remember many nights lying awake in bed listening to your parents yelling and arguing with one another. If your parents were divorced when you were young or were never married, you may have a difficult time even remembering them being together. The truth is that the marriage that was modeled to us through our parents' relationship is, for better or worse, our best teacher of how we relate to our present spouse. Just as we learn (explicitly and implicitly) how to be parents by the way that we were parented, so it is that we learn how to be a husband or a wife by the way that our parents relate to one another. We can either strive to replicate the honor and the devotion that was modeled to us by our parents' relationship, or we can work on having a marriage that is better in a number of ways from the one that our mother and father had with each other. Either way, our goal should be to learn from the strengths and weaknesses of our parents' relationship, and then to take the best and leave the worst as we work on our own marriage.

The reason that a happy marriage is the best gift that you can give to your children is because the relationship between a mom and a dad is the foundation of the home-- the critical piece upon which the rest of the family is built. In any corporation, the success of upper management flows down through the rest of the company, thereby producing a positive work environment and healthy relationships between employers and employees and between one co-worker to another. In the same way, a strong marriage creates a positive family environment and good relationships between one child to another child in the family. When a physical house is built on a firm foundation, it will be able to withstand all kinds of weather conditions. In the same way, when a family is built on a solid marital relationship, it too has the capacity to weather many storms.

Knowing this to be true, how can we put these principles into practice? I believe the first thing that we need to do is to look at how well our marriage is currently functioning.

Exercise 4 – Assessing the Current Quality of Your Marriage

Answer "yes" or "no" to the following questions:

1. Do you feel emotionally connected to your husband the majority of the time?
2. Do you feel loved, respected, and valued by him?
3. Have you and your husband come up with an arrangement that is satisfying to both of you regarding dividing up household chores?
4. Do you feel that your husband supports you in the decisions that you make about your children, your career, or your individual interests?
5. Do you look forward to coming home to your husband, and feel refueled after spending with him?
6. Are you and your husband able to work through conflicts effectively the majority of the time, without withdrawing from one another or having your conversations escalate into big arguments?

Count up the number of questions to which you answered "yes". Believe it or not, it is possible to answer "yes" to all six questions! Each question that you answered "no" to indicates an area in which the quality of your marriage can be improved. It may be time for a "marriage tune-up" from a pastor or a counselor or therapist who specializes in marriage counseling.

You may be surprised by my assertion that it is possible to answer "yes" to all six questions. After all, aren't we supposed to be getting away from the Superwoman image, where even our marriages are perfect? Yes, absolutely! However, the goal of answering "yes" to all six questions does not imply that we need to attain perfection in our marriages. None of the questions address unrealistic goals. Instead, each question identifies a key area in a marriage which needs to be running smoothly in order for a husband and a wife to have a successful relationship, one in which each person is growing together, rather than growing apart. Let's look at each question individually, and break them down into smaller parts so that each area can be examined more closely.

Question 1. Do you feel emotionally connected to your husband the majority of the time?

This first question speaks to the "emotional intimacy" factor in a marriage. For most women, the quality of emotional intimacy is a greater indicator of marital satisfaction than the amount of sexual intimacy. As women, we have been created in such a way that the more emotionally in-tune we feel to our husbands, the more we desire sexual intimacy with them. For us, the desire for sexual intimacy flows naturally out of the emotional connection.

In contrast, for most men, the factor of sexual intimacy is a greater indicator of marital satisfaction than the amount of emotional intimacy. Having a husband's sexual needs met in marriage flows naturally into a man feeling emotionally closer to his wife. It is one of the major ways that men and women are "wired" differently. If we are able to accept and embrace this point, we will be better equipped to understand why our husband's needs may be greater in the area of physical closeness, while our own needs may be greater in the area of emotional closeness. Being emotionally connected to your husband means that the two of you are "in tune" with each other's thoughts and feelings. It implies that you know what is going on with him that is causing him to feel any number of emotions, including happiness, fear, joy, sadness, or anger.

The couples that I have worked with in therapy that have been able to keep this emotional connection strong are those who strive to make a conscious effort to communicate with each other regularly. They realize that if they are not intentionally tuned in and attentive to their spouses, days can easily pass by where the only information exchanged is "business" in nature (e.g., which child needs to be chauffeured to which activity, what time dinner will be that evening, which errands need to be run). We need to connect daily with our husbands as individuals, not just as "business partners" of a corporation. When I catch myself relating to my husband more often as a "roommate" or a "business partner" than as a loving partner, it signals the needs for me to focus on talking with him on a deeper level, realizing that the emotional intimacy of our relationship needs attention. For us, our deep talks frequently occur in the midnight hours, long after the kids are in bed, when one of us initiates conversation about an important issue on our minds. Even after 26 years of marriage, it is important for both of us to remember that we do our relationship a disservice when we presume to already have learned everything there is to know about each other. It is always interesting to hear new things about my husband that I didn't already know, and it's fun to share stories from my past that he hasn't yet heard! This helps us remain emotionally connected to one another.

Question 2: Do you feel loved, respected, and valued by him?

This is a critical piece of a happy marriage, for if we do not feel loved, respected, and valued by our husbands, we will not want to connect with them on either an emotional or a physical basis. Many women I talk to have distanced themselves emotionally from their husbands because they have gotten the message from their spouses that what they say is not important. It is that much more important that we communicate with our spouses when we are feeling unloved, disrespected, or not valued by them.

One book that presents a valuable idea of conceptualizing the different ways that we as individuals prefer to receive and express our love is "The Five Love Languages" by Gary Chapman. In this book, Chapman illustrates five unique ways of communicating love to another person:

a. tangible gifts (e.g. flowers, candy, balloons),
b. acts of service (e.g., cooking dinner, cleaning the house, washing the car),
c. quality time (spending time together),
d. words of affirmation (compliments/ encouragement—either written or spoken), and
e. physical touch (holding hands, hugging, sexual intimacy).

Chapman's premise is that identifying the one or two ways that each of us prefer to receive love can greatly enhance each of our perceptions that we are loved. When we begin to relate to our husbands through their preferred "love language", we will likely be more successful in communicating our love to them. The reverse is also true: when our husbands learn our favorite "love language" and use that method to communicate their feelings to us, we are more likely to feel loved by them.

It might help to understand this concept of "love languages" better with a personal illustration! By going through Gary Chapman's book "The Five Love Languages", my husband and I were able to identify each other's particular "love language". We discovered that his preferred language was "acts of service" and my preferred language was "words of affirmation". By recognizing these differences, I was better able to understand why it was so important for him to have me prepare dinner (even when I am working full-time outside the home and he is a stay-at-home dad!), keep the kitchen clean, or stay current with the laundry. (Hint: It was not because he was a male chauvinist!) In return, he was better able to understand why I valued a comment of, "You look nice today!" over a spotless house or a freshly-vacuumed/waxed/washed car. (Hint: It was not because I was ungrateful!) We simply had different preferences about how we recognized that we are loved. Since I am not certainly not able to do Chapman's book justice by repeating his key points in a few paragraphs, I encourage you and your husband to read "The Five Love Languages" together and see what insight you can obtain from it yourself that might enrich your own marriage.

Question 3: Have you and your husband come up with an arrangement that is satisfying to both of you regarding dividing up household chores?

It has been widely stated that the three most common causes of conflict in marriage are finances, sex, and children. However, it may be safe to assume that a fourth common cause of conflict is housework! When one person feels that he or she has an unfair share of responsibilities in the home, resentment and discontent typically follows. It is less important that the household chores are divided equally, and much more important that each spouse feels that these responsibilities are divided fairly.

Early on in our marriage, my husband and I came up with a mutual agreement/rule. If we were ever bothered by the presence of a household chore (e.g., a sink full of dirty dishes or an overflowing garbage can), then the person who was bothered by it would take care of the problem. This freed us up from nagging the other person to do the chore and put the onus of responsibility on ourselves! I believe that we avoided lots of fights by following this mutual agreement throughout our 26 years of marriage, because many times, what bothered one of us about an unfinished chore did not bother the other person the same way!

An example of this would be my tendency to be a "paper piler". When we were first married, I would frequently stack papers in piles on the kitchen counter, the floor, or any place that had room for piles. This bothered my husband because he has a strong dislike for clutter. His way of taking care of my piles of paper (which he referred to as "clutter"!) was to stuff everything away in drawers, out of sight. The problem with this for me as a person with a "visual" memory was that I could never find what I needed once it had been stuffed away! After discussing this issue together one day, my husband took a large plastic container and labeled it "Sharon's Tub". He proceeded to put in it every piece of paper that I had piled around the house, so that it was all in one place. Then, if I was looking for something that I needed, he would just tell me to look in my "tub". I couldn't complain about the papers being missing, because they were all in one place, and he couldn't complain about the clutter because the countertops were now cleared! What began as his problem of clutter soon became my problem of disorganization, because I spent so much time rooting around in that tub trying to find what I needed! I soon came to learn how to file papers more orderly, so that "Sharon's Tub" is now extinct, and it has been replaced with labeled files in my desk drawer. And there was no nagging or arguing needed to get me there!

If you and your husband find that you often argue about household chores, I encourage the two of you together to break down each task and go through them one-by-one, assigning the task to either yourself or your husband. Then, make a pact that whoever is assigned to that chore will be given permission to do it the way he or she wants to do it, and not have to go through "approval" from the other person about the completeness of the task. This helps to avoid any nagging arguments about "how" someone completed a task. For example, if you cannot live without the dishwasher being stacked a certain way, you should probably sign yourself up for this chore! Otherwise, you will just have to accept the crusted food left on the plates from being jammed too closely together or the Tupperware lids marked "top rack dishwasher safe" that ended up being warped and twisted after being placed on the bottom rack.

Question 4. Do you feel that your husband supports you in the decisions that you make about your children, your career, or your individual interests?

As I mentioned earlier, experts tell us that the three most common areas of unresolved conflict among married couples are sex, children, and money. These are often referred to as "hot button" topics. To have a successful marriage, you and your husband need to agree on these issues. If you are not in agreement, there will be chronic discord in your relationship, which inevitably puts a great deal of strain on your marriage.

When it comes to parenting, we are most influenced by the way that we were parented in our own families of origin. The challenge of this is that much of our influences

occur on a level at which we are not consciously aware.
For example, in some families, sleepovers for kids at their
friends' houses are commonplace and occur frequently.
In other families, children are only allowed to spend the
night with a limited number of friends, and only when
those friends and their families know each other quite well.
Both of these ways of managing sleepovers are acceptable,
but they may create a source of conflict between you and
your husband if you each grew up with a differing set of
rules about children spending the night away from home.
Our individual expectations that we bring to our marriage
about these and many other parenting issues need to be
explored and discussed with our spouses so that there is
general consensus regarding how these are to be managed.

Children thrive in families where parents display a
"united front" when it comes to the areas of setting limits,
boundaries, rules, and discipline. It is a child's nature to
try to "play off" one parent against the other in order to
get what a child wants. If you and your husband do not
agree on parenting issues, your children will be able to
wedge their way between you and manipulate outcomes
of situations to their advantage. What can result is an
unbalanced family hierarchy where a child is aligned more
with one parent instead of each parent being most strongly
aligned with one another. Here is an example of how this
may play out in a family: Joey and Mom "team up" against
Dad because both believe that Dad is "too strict". As a
result, Mom indulges Joey in activities that Dad would
not allow in an effort to compensate for Dad's perceived
rigidity. Consequently, Mom and Dad have frequent
arguments about whose parenting style is "right".

A better way of managing these differences in permissiveness would be for Mom and Dad to discuss privately what activities they will and will not allow Joey to participate in, come to an acceptable compromise between themselves on this issue, and then support each other outwardly in front of Joey by saying something like, "Your Dad and I don't think you should go to that all-night lock-in at the school." In this way, Mom and Dad do not allow Joey to use their different levels of permissiveness to his advantage.

It is equally important that you and your husband support one another when it comes to careers. A mutual decision must be made regarding whose career should take priority at which stage of your family's life cycle. There are several stages to the life cycle of a family:

Family Life Cycle

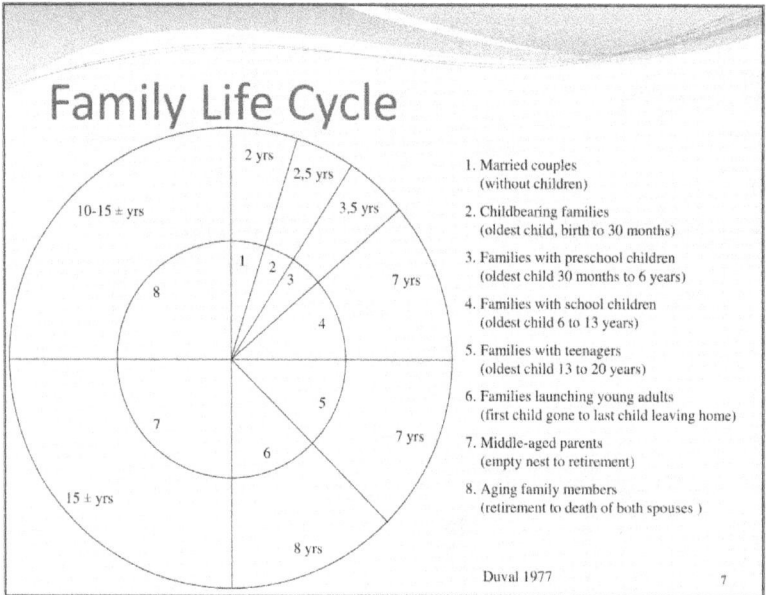

1. Married couples
   (without children)
2. Childbearing families
   (oldest child, birth to 30 months)
3. Families with preschool children
   (oldest child 30 months to 6 years)
4. Families with school children
   (oldest child 6 to 13 years)
5. Families with teenagers
   (oldest child 13 to 20 years)
6. Families launching young adults
   (first child gone to last child leaving home)
7. Middle-aged parents
   (empty nest to retirement)
8. Aging family members
   (retirement to death of both spouses)

Duval 1977

-being newly married

-being married without children

-raising infants

-raising toddlers/preschoolers

-raising elementary-aged children

-raising teenagers

-becoming empty nesters

-parenting adult children

-grandparenting

It may be helpful to look at these different stages when evaluating careers of you and your husband, because priorities of careers often change as your family's life cycle changes and it is important that each of you remain flexible in finding what works best for your family. For example, before our children started school, my husband and I felt strongly that we wanted to be the ones to take care of our children, rather than having them go to daycare. In order for us to do this at the same time that we each pursued our own careers, we juggled our schedules so that one of us was always home with the kids. He would go to work from 8:00 a.m. to 4:00 p.m. and then when he came home, I would head out the door for work from 5:00 p.m. to 9:00 p.m. I also worked on Saturdays when he was home with the children, and at one point, on Wednesdays, when he would telecommute from home. What we gained was being able to balance both our jobs we well as being home with our kids, but what became more challenging was creating time to spend with one another.

However, our family moved to a different stage of the family life cycle when all three of our kids were in school all day. My husband was then at home full-time because of chronic pain from a back disability, while I altered my schedule and began working outside of the home full-time as the primary breadwinner for our family. We then had much more time to spend together, both as a couple and as a family, but we also moved into a different set of challenges.

While our boys were in high school and college, our family had an even more non-traditional home life. My husband and our youngest son moved to Florida so that our youngest son could pursue his goal of obtaining a college basketball scholarship. I lived at our home in Ohio where our middle son and I helped take care of my husband's mother who was blind and in the end stages of renal disease. She received peritoneal dialysis which we provided for her at home on a nightly basis. Our oldest son was away at college at the time and only came home during the summer. It was just one more example of a crazy season of family life for us!

Speaking of family life, one of my biggest pet peeves is the constant "mommy wars" that are frequently waged between stay-at-home moms and "working" moms (i.e., those that work outside the home). Each side seems to constantly try to justify why their decision is the "best" one while they inevitably criticize the other side's choices. The reason that I hate this debate is that I know that there is really no one "best" choice that can be applied unilaterally to all mothers, and that each choice has its own share of benefits and challenges. I know this because I have done them all! I have stayed at home full-time, worked outside of the home part-time, and worked outside of the home full-time. The issues of balancing schedules, fighting "mommy guilt", finding "couples' time", meeting the needs of children, striving for personal fulfillment, and managing finances were always present, regardless of which way I divided my time at home versus my time at work; what changed were the solutions that were devised to address these problems.

One last point to bring up that relates to Question Four is that it is important for every married couple to also come up with a way to balance each person's individual interests and activities, taking into consideration the amount of time, money, and energy that is spent on these activities. Resentment can quickly build in a marriage when one spouse attempts to continue to pursue his or her own interests with the same intensity as he or she did before being married and having children. An example of this would be one spouse playing for a softball league that practices two evenings a week and has games lasting several hours every weekend, to the extent that the family feels neglected and misses that parent's presence in family activities. In order to make something like this work, both spouses must be in agreement that a time-intensive individual activity like this is a good one.

Question 5. Do you look forward to coming home to your husband (or your husband coming home to you) and feel refueled after spending time with him?

My husband and I have always talked about wanting our home to be a "sanctuary"--a place where we could retreat to when the world was making us weary. In addition, we enjoy coming home to each other to "rest and retreat" from outside stressors. Just about every night, one of us says to the other, "It's good to be married", and we mean it! We are best friends, as well as marriage partners, and we enjoy just being together. Lest you think our marriage is too idealistic, let me assure you that we still get on each other's nerve at times! We just do our best to communicate to each other that we are feeling irritable and need some time alone. After 26 years of marriage, I think we're finally getting to the point where we can give (and receive!) this message without taking it (too) personally!

I am consciously aware that "workaholics" are created not only by one's love for his or her job or career, but also by a wish to avoid the time and energy involved in maintaining relationships with one's spouse and one's children. We all need to ask ourselves, "Do I look forward to going to work more than I look forward to coming home?" and then commit to giving ourselves an honest answer to that question. If it's coming home that we find ourselves wanting to avoid, then we need to evaluate how to improve things at home so that we can look with anticipation towards coming home, rather than with dread.

When one spouse stays home and takes care of the kids all day, that person is left to the mercy of little creatures who depend on the parent for every diaper change, feeding, drink, and type of entertainment. The days' jobs of preparing meals, cleaning up messes, and breaking up sibling arguments can be monotonous and tedious. It is not uncommon for the stay-at-home parent to find him or herself exhausted, emotionally and physically drained, craving adult conversation, or just needing "alone time" at the end of the day.

I remember one mom telling me that when she was with her kids at home all day when they were young, all she wanted to do some nights when her husband got home was just leave the house and wander up and down the aisles of Wal-Mart! Marriages that understand the dynamics of these needs are better at being responsive and flexible to each other.

In turn, the spouse with a job outside the home often spends his or her day solving problems, interacting with adults, returning phone calls, checking e-mails, and tending to things at the office. In order to be successful on the job, this spouse needs to be able to separate the concerns from home with the issues confronting him or her at work. I learned this first-hand when I returned to work for a few hours a week in my private practice after my third child was born: I had to be able to separate both physically and emotionally from my children in order to focus my attention on my clients and their needs. It made me realize for the first time what it must be like for fathers who return to work shortly after their babies are born. They have to focus on the role of being the breadwinner and provider for the family and cannot give in to the feelings of sadness and separation anxiety that comes with being away from a new baby. If dads were not able to "contain" these feelings, they would not be able to leave home and go to work, and what we would find would be that parents would not be able to earn a living after having children because neither of them would be able to survive emotionally when they were away from their babies!

My point in all this is to raise your awareness of what you and your spouse goes through each day, whether staying at home or going off to work. It is imperative that in order to maintain a healthy marriage, we must be sensitive to the other's person's struggles.

Take a moment to answer the following questions for yourself:

- Do you actively take part in planning "date nights" with your husband at least once a month?

- Do you plan overnight "getaways" (without the kids!) at least once a year?

- Do you try your best to spend time on a daily basis communicating with your husband one-on-one, and learning from one another what each other's day was like?

These are all ways that we can actively work towards preventing what I call "marriage drift". When managing a household with children, it is easy for parents to get caught up in the busyness of day-to-day activities and lose sight of the intimacy of their marriage relationship. It may feel like the two of you are "business partners" rather than husband and wife. Although it seems like we have children in our home for much of our lives, in reality it is actually just a small time in the life of a marriage. For example, a couple who gets married at age 25 and has two children who are three years apart after they have been married for a couple of years will have over 30 years of their married life together after their youngest child turns

18! This emphasizes the importance of staying emotionally connected to your spouse. Sadly, many couples turn to each other after their children are raised, only to discover that they have drifted apart and the only thing that was keeping them together was child-rearing.

Another clue that the two of you may not be connecting intimately with each other is when information exchanged between the two of you is mostly about the "business details" of your family (e.g. who needs a ride where, or whether or not the field trip money has been sent to the school) and less about the emotional matters (e.g. what happened in each other's lives that has prompted feelings of joy or discouragement). When our children were young, my father consistently stressed to us the importance of my husband and I planning regular "date nights". We had to make an agreement on our date nights that we would only spend the first 15 minutes or so talking about the kids, and then the rest of the night any conversation about the kids was considered off-limits! It forced us to develop our relationship in talking about other areas.

One way to stay connected is for you and your husband to ask each other in the morning (or the night before) if there is anything that the other person can think of that you can pray for them about that day. Maybe your husband is dreading a 10:00 a.m. meeting with an important client, or maybe you are anxious about a performance review that day. Making a conscious effort of asking each other for your daily prayer requests and then carrying them out at certain times of the day is a great way to stay emotionally connected. It also offers information that you can then follow-up with each other that evening when you are both at home together again. Stormie Omartian offers many great ideas on how to pray for your spouse in her books, "The Power of a Praying Wife" and "The Power of a Praying Husband".

Question 6: Are you and your husband able to work through conflicts effectively the majority of the time without withdrawing from one another or having your conversations escalate into big arguments?

This last question is an important one, as successful conflict resolution is an essential characteristic of healthy marriages. Dr. John Gottman and his colleagues have done a great deal of research on the essential ingredients of happy marriages. They found that one of the critical determining factors of which marriages stay together and which marriages end in divorce has to do with how the couples resolved conflict. It is imperative in any marriage that each couple find ways to resolve conflict successfully. Spouses that are able to talk through problems effectively and resolve differences in healthy ways (including agreeing to disagree!) continue to grow together, rather than grow apart. Knowing the rules for "fighting fair" can go a long way towards resolving conflict successfully.

Here is a handout that I created for couples on "fighting fair":

Guidelines for 'Fighting Fair"
by Dr. Sharon Phillips

1. Timing is everything--
Pick an appropriate time for a discussion. Avoid times when people are hungry, tired, in a hurry, or otherwise preoccupied in some way.

2. Be specific---
Use examples when available to clarify your point. Avoid the use of overgeneralizations such as "always" and "never".

3. Keep your cool--
Keep your emotions from controlling your communication. If you find yourself getting too angry or upset, agree to take a "break" from the conversation for a specific period of time, and come up with a rescheduled time to continue the discussion.

4. Stay on topic--
Avoid going off on tangents, or bringing up other points that are only vaguely related to the topic of discussion.

5. Be constructive, not destructive--
Avoid defensiveness in yourself and the other person by voicing your opinion about another's behavior or actions, and not attacking another's "character". Try to keep an open mind to "constructive criticism", rather than becoming defensive.

6. Don't hit "below the belt"--
It is never good to pick on another person's weak spots, just because you know what they are.

7. Work together as a team--

Keep the goal of any discussion as problem-solving and solution-finding, rather than believing one person has to be right and the other one, wrong.

8. Agree to disagree--

It is not necessary to see "eye-to-eye" on everything in relationships.

9. Avoid "communication stoppers"--

Examples of these include withdrawing, hanging up, or walking away. If it is necessary to stop the discussion, make this clear to the other person and reschedule another time to continue the conversation.

10. Let each person talk--

Allow each person to have his/her say. No one likes to be interrupted.

11. "Enough already"--

Come up with a signal to let the other person know you understand his/her point, so it does not have to be repeated "ad nauseum". A verbal "I got your point" or a nonverbal hand sign can be effective.

12. Restate the obvious--

Let the other person know when you've understood them by saying, "What I hear you saying is...." and repeat it back to them. Give the other person a chance to correct you if you misheard them, and then repeat it back once again to them.

There are many, many books that have been written on resolving conflict, and if you and your husband find that you need to develop more skills in this area, it will likely benefit the two of you to read one or more of these books with each other (a sampling which can be found at the end of this section) or from seeing a marriage therapist together.

Chapter 5

Plate 2b: Having Quantity and Quality Time with Your Children

We've all heard the distinction made between "quality" time and "quantity" time, and we've probably also taken part in the debate about which is more important when it comes to spending time with our kids. This debate is closely related to the "Mommy Wars" described in the last chapter, where stay-at-home moms are pitted against moms that work outside the home, in an attempt to determine which position is the best one for the children. As the debate often goes, stay-at-home moms argue that they have more "quantity" time with their children since their kids are not in daycare, and often assert that this "quantity" time is what is most important when it comes to raising our kids. In defense, moms that work outside of the home often stress that the time that they can offer their children is "quality" time, since these moms have more limited time to spend with their children, and therefore they work harder at making those moments special.

As I stated in an earlier chapter, my reaction to these arguments is that when it comes down to it, BOTH quality AND quantity time are essential in raising emotionally healthy children. In my opinion, folks engaged in these "Mommy Wars" just need to quit fighting and trying to "one-up" the other side. Balance is what is most important here.

Children need us to spend "quantity" time with them, where we might not be doing anything of earth-shattering importance, but we are working with them shoulder-to-shoulder. Examples of quantity time might be cleaning the house together, working in the yard together, sitting around watching T.V. together, or going grocery shopping together. These hours spent together might not seem important, but they are all investments in the relationship between you and your children. It is during this "quantity" time that we are teaching them how to tend to necessary tasks and modeling for our kids how to involve the whole family in activities that might not necessarily be fun but are essential parts of life.

In addition, children also need us to spend "quality" time with them—time that has as its main focus getting to know your child better, being a coach or an encourager for your child, or just enjoying life's simple pleasures together. Examples of quality time would be taking turns spending one-on-one time with each child doing an activity of the child's choice (i.e. "Mommy dates" or "Daddy dates"), reading to your child at bedtime, camping out in the backyard together, or having a picnic in the park and throwing a baseball to one another. "Quality" time with our children sends them the message that "You are important" and frees us from the pressure of having to "get things done". The most important part of "quality" time is focusing your attention on your child and just enjoying him or her during those moments.

We spoke earlier about the different stages of the life cycle of a family, from being newly married to grandparenting. In a similar way, it is important to look at the developmental stage of your child when trying to figure out how to meets his or her needs of quality and quantity time. Just as families have different needs and priorities based on what stage of the family life cycle they are in, so do children have different needs for quantity and quality time based on their ages and developmental stages.

Infants rely on us for their every need. We are there to feed them, clothe them, diaper them, bathe them, soothe them, and entertain them. Our "quantity" time with them involves meeting all their physical needs, which is pretty comprehensive! Meeting a baby's physical needs helps meet their emotional needs of healthy attachment and development of trust. When infants discover that their cries result in our attention to their needs, they build trust that the world is a safe place, and they begin to form healthy attachments to their caregivers. Our "quality" time with our children when they are babies involves holding, rocking, cuddling, snuggling, entertaining, and spoiling them. It includes letting them have "floor time" and exposing them to different stimuli and environments.

Toddlers are beginning to be more independent as they acquire skills of walking and talking but are still highly dependent on us as parents. There is still quite a bit of our "quantity" time that is needed, such as to provide food for them, help them with their clothes, potty train them, bathe them, soothe them, and help entertain them. Our "quality" time with toddlers involves accompanying them and ensuring their safety as they begin to explore the fascinating world around them.

Preschoolers have begun to be able to separate from us for longer periods of time. Preschool environments offer opportunities for young children to develop their social skills and to begin to follow the structure of a learning environment. When are children are preschool-aged, "quantity" time can be spent teaching them simple chores at home as they learn the importance of contributing to the family. "Quantity" time also involves continuing to offer them a high degree of appropriate supervision, along with encouraging their budding independence. "Quality" time can include creating soothing rituals with them for bedtime and focusing on the individual gifts, talents, and interests that your preschooler is beginning to display.

Elementary-aged children spend a large part of their days in structured learning environments, whether traditionally schooled or homeschooled. Their main tasks are to further improve friendship skills, develop a love for learning, attain achievements in areas important to them, and discover new interests and passions. Elementary-aged children need "quantity" time with us in order to observe how we respond in different situations and to be influenced by our model of how we react to others.

"Quantity" time can also be important in learning more about our children's friends as we chaperone some of their various group activities.

For the elementary-aged group, "quality" time conveys a strong message that we as parents are interested in continuing to learn about their likes and dislikes, strengths and "growing edges", interests and abilities. Ideas for spending "quality' time with grade-schoolers include working on projects like arts and crafts or science activities together, having a picnic in the park, spending the day one-on-one with your child, or baking cookies together.

Junior high kids are known to be both clingy as well as fiercely independent. As their bodies are being transformed during puberty, the rushing surge of their hormones contributes to a budding self-consciousness and a rollercoaster ride of emotions which makes it quite challenging indeed for middle school children to navigate through this stage of their life. (I often quote to the parents of middle school kids, "Nobody has ever told me that they wish they could be 13 again!") In addition, junior high kids have the daunting tasks of figuring out where they fit in the social "pecking order" that exists in school, managing lockers and increasingly complex projects and assignments, figuring out the varying expectations of different teacher for each class, and learning to balance their time effectively between academic and extracurricular activities. Our junior high kids need "quantity" time with us as we carry out mundane household tasks together so that they can develop responsibility and benefit from the gifts of consistency and interdependence that families can offer. Our "quantity" time can be spent teaching our children how to do laundry, how to prepare a meal for the family, and how to clean up afterwards! Middle school children also need "quality" time with us so that we can continue to keep the lines of communication flowing between parent and teen as they challenge the beliefs and opinions from others around them and begin to choose which of these they will keep for their own. "Quality" time can include an afternoon shopping together, working with a young teen on his or her science fair project, or grabbing some ice cream or a smoothie together.

High school teens may act like they don't need either "quantity" OR "quality" time with us, but don't let their façade fool you! (I'm reminded of the popular public service advertisement on television that ends with the phrase, "They still need you to be their parents.") I often told the parents of the teens I worked with to think of their high school kids as going through an older version of "toddlerhood", complete with temper tantrums, emotional outbursts, and vacillating degrees of independence and "wanting Mommy". Indeed, the developmental tasks of high school kids are similar to toddlers: the quest for independence ("Put me down!" and "I can do it myself!") coupled with the need for a secure home base to which they can return ("Pick me up!" and "I need help!"). Our high school kids need "quantity" time to help them acquire the required hours of driving time needed to obtain their license, to help them navigate college applications and schedule doctor physicals, and to teach them that even when they rear their "surly monster heads", we still love them and want them to be a part of our family. Our "quality" time with our high school children can be spent catching up on their lives over a latte or a pizza, making ourselves available for late-night talks as needed, and seeking their ideas on how to improve things at home or in the world around them.

As our youngsters grow into young adults and leave for college or their own apartments, our "quantity" and "quality" time may often feel like we are spending time with our same-aged peers. While we always need to continue to keep appropriate emotional boundaries with our young adult children (e.g. not confide in them about challenges we might encounter in our marriage), it is healthy for us as parents of this age group to offer greater degrees of self-disclosure about what we struggled with when we were their age. By virtue of our children now being young adults, we may naturally find that there are many more opportunities for "quality" time than there are for "quantity" time, as our young adult children continue to develop more independent lives of their own. I am struck by the contrast of this description where we may experience a lopsidedness of more quality time with young adults, as compared to the lopsidedness of more quantity time that we had with them when they were infants. Such is the cycle of life!

It is also important to keep in mind that we may be naturally skilled or feel a "goodness of fit" between our own personalities and skills sets and the seasons of life that our children go through. As a personal example, I was surprised at how much I did not exactly enjoy the baby/toddler ages of my children. (I'm sure part of that had to do with having 3 children in 4 years!) Since I had loved babysitting when I was a tween and teen myself, I thought it would only make sense that I would love having babies of my own even more! Don't get me wrong, I did love my children when they were babies, I was just surprised to find myself exhausted (either physically, mentally, or emotionally) a great deal of the time! (I also had sleep apnea that went undiagnosed until my children were much older, which likely contributed to my fatigue at the time.) It only occurred to me later that one important difference is that when I was a teenage babysitter, my job ended once I put the kids to bed, and I didn't have interrupted nights and too-early mornings when I babysat because I always went back to my own home and slept in my own bed, all night, undisturbed. I never realized how important sleep was to me until I became a parent!

On the brighter side, what also surprised me about parenting is how much I enjoyed parenting teenagers! I'd heard (as I'm sure many of you have heard) that parenting teens was one of many people's least favorite ages/stages, and therefore I expected that this would also be true of me. However, what I did discover about myself was quite the opposite—I loved being the mother of teenage boys! As teenagers, our boys were funny, helpful, and ready to engage in all kinds of discussions, as well as continually educated me on pop culture and the latest slang!

Exercise 5—How Developmental Stages of Your Children Affect Your Interactions with Your Kids:

This exercise will assist you in identifying the developmental stages of your children and how you can best target your quality and quantity time with each of them. Fill out the table on the next page for each of your children. When completing the information under the headings of "quality and quantity time ideas", keep in mind your child's unique talents, gifts, interests, abilities, skills, and personality characteristics. These ideas can be very different for each child, based upon all these distinct variables.

Child's Name	Age	Developmental Stage (e.g. high school)	Quality Time Ideas

Chapter 6

Plate 3: Excelling at Work

One of the most memorable quotes I ever heard regarding work was from my clinical supervisor at the first job I held after receiving my doctorate in psychology. She said, "Work is a part of life—work is not life." This was very helpful to me as I started my career, and it has echoed in my mind at various times throughout my life since then. I think this quote is particularly relevant to this book, which is all about balance, and this chapter is about balancing work with the other "plates" in our lives.

One thing to keep in mind is that work will play a different role for us in relation to the different seasons we have in our families. Remember back in Chapter Four when we spoke about the different seasons that families go through based upon the changing ages and stages of their children? I believe that when striving to keep our lives to be in balance, it may work best for our work to also change as our families' lives change. My husband and I have talked about this many times over the years. We felt strongly that the time in our lives when our kids were at home was the time for my own career to take off and flourish, as I expanded my private practice and spent time in writing and speaking engagements. With this agreement about the different peak times for our various careers in mind, we are able to work together in unison and collaborate on decisions that lead to these goals.

In general, overall my challenge has been to balance my work with the other plates in my life. I have remarked to my clients in the past that when you love what you do, it can be tempting to let your work consume your life, but that if you don't like your job, you are never in any danger of becoming a workaholic! When I was growing up, my father used to frequently say that getting paid to do what you love to do is the best career of all. I would have to agree with him about that. My dad truly felt passionate about his job as a teacher, and you could see his whole face light up whether he was in front of his classroom or just working one-on-one trying to impart some knowledge about math or computers.

I feel very blessed to have discovered my true calling for my life's profession while I was still a junior in high school. It was that year that I took a psychology course and found out that I really enjoyed the topic. I had always been fascinated with people and their life stories, and even when I was in elementary school, I preferred reading stories about real people as opposed to stories about talking animals in forests! In that first psychology class, I found that the words and terms used to describe the concepts of psychology came easily to me and stuck in my mind.

When I later enrolled at Xavier University as a freshman, I had narrowed down my career choices to becoming either a pediatrician or a child psychologist. The one thing that I knew for sure was that I wanted to work with children. I took a couple of pre-med classes my freshman year and discovered that the hard-core science classes required for a career in medicine were definitely not my forte. I decided to declare my major in psychology. And, as they say, the rest is history!

Even though I have dedicated the first part of my life's work to improving the emotional lives of children as a child psychologist, I made a commitment to myself early on that I did not want to spend all my time working with other people's children at the expense of neglecting time with my own children. When I built my private practice years ago, I was blessed with the freedom to make my own schedule. (However, being self-employed also has its share of challenges, and whenever I overscheduled myself, my husband was fond of saying, "You should complain to your boss!".) Since I worked primarily with children and families at the time, the demand for my time was heaviest during after-school hours and on weekends, when kids were out of school. I learned at that time that it was essential that I set firm boundaries on my schedule, because when my own children were not in school, they also needed me to spend some of that time at home with them. There have been many times that I have felt pressure from the families that I worked with to expand my hours to meet their scheduling needs, but I tried to remember that I could work every evening until 9:00 p.m. and every Saturday and Sunday all weekend long, and still have more families wanting more of my time. It helps me to remember that my main priority is my family, and then work follows after that.

Sticking to these priorities has been invaluable when there are scheduling conflicts that pit time at work against time with family. When my kids were still at home, I tried to do my best to arrange my hours (even occasionally having to change things previously scheduled) so that I was available to my family for parent-teacher conferences, open houses at school, sporting games, and other important events. Again, it worked well for me to arrange my work schedule differently based upon my family's needs at the time (hint: here is another reference to family "seasons"!). Over the years, I have changed my work hours in different ways in order to accommodate our family. There have been seasons where I worked all day on Saturdays and took Fridays off. At other times, I have worked one late night a week until 8:00 p.m. or even 9:00 p.m.

For many summers when I had my private practice focused on kids and families, I enjoyed keeping a more "traditional" workday of 9:00 a.m. – 5:00 p.m. three days a week, working one "late night" per week until 8:00 p.m., and then taking three-day weekends throughout most of the summer. At that time, I liked changing my hours in the summer to more "daytime" hours to take advantage of children being able to come for therapy during the day since they were out of school for the summer. In return, my family and I were rewarded with long weekends, frequently spent camping in different places in our RV. It was wonderful to be home to enjoy those long evenings of sunshine in the summer, and I didn't even mind working later in the evenings that much once the time changed and the days grew shorter and colder.

You may be reading this and thinking, "That's great for you, Sharon. But my situation with work is different." True, but I believe there are likely to be some variables in your job that can be changed, and it is up to you to determine what parts of your job are working well for you and what aren't, and then strive to come up with some solutions to balance your time and energy more effectively, in a way that brings you peace and joy. The following exercise may help you to do just that.

Exercise 6—Looking at Your Role as an Employee: How Satisfied are You?

Circle True or False for the following statements.

1. T/F I am satisfied with the number of hours I work per week.
2. T/F There is nothing that I would change about my work schedule.
3. T/F I feel appropriately challenged in my job.
4. T/F I look forward to going to work most days.
5. T/F I enjoy the majority of interactions I have with my coworkers.
6. T/F I feel that I am paid appropriately for my job.
7. T/F I find my work enjoyable most of the time.
8. T/F With few exceptions, I do not feel the need to bring my work home with me.
9. T/F I feel that my job is in line with my interests or my passions.

10. T/F I do not often find myself thinking about what it would be like to work somewhere else.

For each item to which you answered False, take a few minutes to examine your answer more closely and use the following questions to help:

a. Is this a new complaint or a more longstanding one?

b. Is this an issue that will likely resolve itself in the near future or is it something that I need to be more proactive about changing?

c. Could anything be changed at work to help with this problem?

d. Is there anyone I know that feels good about this issue in their own job that could perhaps give me some advice on changing this issue in my job?

e. Is there another job or position in my field or another field that would bring me more joy or satisfaction? What are the steps that I would need to take towards this other job or position? When might I be able to begin taking those steps?

Even if you aren't presently working outside the home, a history of work is something we are likely to all have in common: it is the rare individual, indeed, who has never held down a paid job. It may have been many years since you landed your first part-time job (mine was at Baskin-Robbins ice cream store, where I gained 10 pounds in one summer at age 16, but that is a story for another day!) and you may have not worked outside the home since you had children, but at some point in time, most women have had the experience of being an employee. It is these shared experiences that I would like to focus on, and not the debate of whether it is more important to be a stay-at-home mom as opposed to being a mother who works outside the home. (If you have not already picked up on this, I view the "mommy wars" as quite useless). I strongly believe that whether staying at home full-time, working outside of the home full-time, or working at a job part-time, all mothers face similar challenges. Regardless of a mom's working "status", we all must make choices about where to spend our time, how to spend our time, and in what ways we will accomplish our many obligations.

I'd like to take a moment and look at the many benefits that women derive from holding a job. Among them, being a paid employee helps us to:

- develop time management skills,

- improve our ability to work with different types of people,

- showcase our unique talents and gifts,

- contribute financially to our families,

- model for our children the values of holding a job,

- receive feedback based upon how well we are performing in our work,

- feel that we are contributing to a good greater than ourselves and our families,

- avoid feelings of isolation and loneliness,

- meet others with whom we share common interests and goals.

You may be able to identify other ways that working benefits you. What is one of the top reasons that you chose to have one of your jobs (either a job you currently have now, or one you have had in the past)? Write the reason here:

_____

_____

_____

_____

_____

_____

One of the first benefits I listed above is that being an employee helps us develop time management skills. Boy, isn't that the truth! (We can say that becoming a mother does the same thing, right??) Regardless of the position you hold, we are all granted the same 24 hours in a day. Some people say that we need more hours in the day, but I believe that if that were the case, we mothers would still fall short of getting all that we want or need to get done. It's a truism that work expands to fill the time allotted to it. I don't know about you, but I often am more productive when I am busy. Too much time on my hands sometimes leads me to become lazy and unmotivated. As with anything, there is a balance, and feeling overly stressed and pressed for time at work is a sure sign to me that I need to reallocate my work duties.

"Work smarter, not harder" is a saying that I try to keep in mind. By managing my time more efficiently, I can often get more work done in a shorter period of time. One of the tips I try to practice which helps me with effective time management at work is to break up longer periods of work with short breaks. Research has proven that our minds are designed to hold maximum attention for no longer than 45 minutes at a time. After 45 minutes, our brains tend to drift, and we lose our focus and our concentration. Even though we might still be on task, after focusing our attention for 45 consecutive minutes, we are less efficient. I like to follow the tip given to top executives of Fortune 500 companies: work diligently for 45 minutes, then take a break for 15 minutes by getting up from your desk, stretching, chatting with a colleague, or going outside. You will find that you are more productive in 3 hours by taking a 15-minute break every 45 minutes than you would be if you worked 3 hours straight without stopping at all. Try it and see! If during your 45 minutes of work, you find your mind wandering to other tasks you need to do instead, then just keep a sheet of paper nearby and jot down the tasks so you don't forget them and wait until your next 15-minute break to tackle them. Put your cell phone aside, and don't allow yourself to be distracted for those 45 minutes of uninterrupted time; return phone calls and check e-mails during your 15-minute breaks.

Being an employee also helps us improve our interpersonal relationship skills. Who among us hasn't been challenged to interact effectively with a particularly "prickly" person? By "prickly", I mean people that are difficult to work with. They might be bossy, lazy, slackers, overly demanding, grumpy, negative, gossipy—you name it! Whatever the case might be, when you are forced to work with people with these qualities, you have an opportunity to hone your interpersonal skills. It's easy to be nice to nice people; the real challenge is to work well with prickly people (without becoming prickly yourself!) Some things that help me in working with prickly people are:

- to focus on business, rather than getting caught up in emotion,

- to look at these individuals as being unhappy people who need my sympathy, rather than mean people who are "out to get me", and

- to point out some of the difficulties with the process of our communication, rather than just focusing on the content of the discussions. (For example, "It seems that every time you ask me for advice, you shoot down all the ideas that I offer you. Is there something else you are looking for from me instead?")

If you need help in dealing effectively with prickly people, you might find it beneficial to refer to some of the resources at the end of this book that focus on communication skills or handling difficult interpersonal relationships. This is one area in which I am grateful to have a background in psychology, because so much of our training focuses on learning how to interact effectively with others. These skills are invaluable in dealing with others in everyday situations—from speaking to the clerk at the grocery store to interacting with the server taking my order at lunch. I encourage you to further develop your skills in interpersonal communication if dealing with prickly people is a daunting task for you.

In my opinion, one of the most exciting benefits of having a paid job is having the opportunity to showcase your unique talents and gifts. Remember earlier when

I shared that getting paid to do something you love is (as American Express commercials say) "priceless"? In reflecting upon this fact, what came to my mind are the many women I know who have developed businesses out of their individual talents such as:

- painting children's murals on nursery walls
- designing gift baskets
- creating quilts and other crafts
- making lotions and creams from essential oils
- cleaning homes
- baking cookies
- putting on plays for children at local elementary schools
- photography
- performing music at weddings
- catering
- giving lessons (piano, sewing, using the computer, dance, aerobics)
- providing childcare to help other working mothers
- organizing other people's homes.

Really, the possibilities are endless! If this thought intrigues you, answer the following questions:

1. People have told me that I am really good at

_____

_____

2. Something that I really enjoy and would do even if I didn't get paid to do it is

_____

_____

3. There are times when I hear this still, small voice within me say that I could be really good at

_____

_____

If you don't feel ready to branch out on your own, you might want to consider becoming a part of a larger company that focuses on women entrepreneurs. Some of the more well-known companies are Avon, Mary Kay, Pampered Chef, Tastefully Simple, Southern Living at Home, Thirty-One, and Premier Designs Jewelry.

Obviously, one of the key advantages to holding a paid position is to be able to contribute financially to our families. There is a great amount of personal satisfaction that can be derived from directly generating your own income. In considering paid employment, we've probably all heard the discussion about the need to factor in costs associated with working, such as transportation costs, wardrobe expenses, and daycare needs for our children. What is less likely talked about but is equally important to keep in mind, is the "hidden" costs associated with working outside of the home, such as the emotional toll of demands on the job (like dealing with "prickly" people!), the challenge of keeping up with household tasks, being away from your family, and the "fatigue" factor of having a job.

If you have decided that in the present season of your family's life, it is important for you to be a stay-at-home mom, you may receive validation from the following statistic gathered from www.salary.com (2024) which estimates the value of jobs handled by a stay-at-home parent to be $184,820 per year! This reflects a 106-hour work week and takes into account wages from jobs that are normally provided by several other occupations, including but not limited to: logistics analyst, judge/magistrate, childcare worker, housekeeper, chauffeur, cook, and personal assistant. That's a considerable salary!

Another benefit to holding a paid position is that we can model for our children the values of holding a job. We are teaching them the importance of responsibility, commitment, and a strong work ethic (as evidenced by the days we show up to work even when we don't feel like going!). We are showing them through our actions that people with jobs have lives, too! Remember how when we were younger, we thought our teachers lived at school? It was hard for us to imagine that they were mothers and fathers with their own families and homes away from school. This was also seen at times in my private practice, where my office included a couch, chairs, an armoire (packed with toys and games), and a small fridge. On more than one occasion, children have inquired, "Do you live here?", to which I sometimes replied, "No, but sometimes I feel like I do!"

In my experience, two of the most frustrating parts of being a mother of young children are the monotony of the job (feed, nap, clean...repeat!) and the lack of feedback I received about how I was doing. Small children never say, "Gee, Mom, thanks so much for cleaning up all of my messes and changing my diaper so many times today!" As a result, I had to find my own way of positively reinforcing and praising myself that I had done a good job that day as a mother. In contrast, when we are employees or business owners, we have much more tangible ways to receive feedback based upon how well we are performing in our work. We can see the positive results of increased sales, improved productivity, or higher numbers of customers. We may even receive merit raises based on our performance! (Imagine that being the case in our role as mothers!) This is a valuable aspect of holding a job.

Being an employee can also help us feel that we are contributing to a greater good than ourselves and our families. If our jobs consist of dealing with the public, we can have the satisfaction of knowing that we have affected someone else's life in a positive way. Working outside the home can help give us a perspective on the world in general, and how we are really a small part of the greater scheme of things. When I stayed at home with young children, I found it to be so easy to get trapped in the narrow mindset that a clean house was the end-all, be-all of life! As a child psychologist, I was reminded regularly of the challenges that other people face in their daily lives, and it frequently prompted me to go home and hug my children and be grateful for the love of my spouse and the warmth of my home.

Work provides us with the opportunity to avoid feelings of isolation and loneliness. True, there are some jobs where people work more independently and individually, but for the most part, there is often some interaction with other people. One thing I missed most during the days I stayed at home when my children were young was an uninterrupted lunch hour! Being a psychologist in private practice is unique in that you work with people all day yet can still feel very isolated from your therapist colleagues, because everyone is behind their own closed doors working with clients! On my lunch break, I looked forward to getting out of the office, grabbing my current reading material (a favorite book or magazine) and relaxing at a nearby restaurant. It was then that I could refuel my soul and feel refreshed.

The last benefit of working outside the home that I wanted to mention was the opportunity to meet others with whom we share common interests and goals. Certainly, one can argue that this same benefit can be acquired from gathering with other mothers, even if you are not employed. I believe this to be true, and perhaps it is one benefit that can be found both in staying at home and in working outside of the home.

Chapter 7

Plate 4: Succeeding in School

When my kids used to fret that they had to study for a test for school, I would always assure them that I was more than qualified to help them learn how to study since I went to school for 21 years! I've certainly taken my share of tests and quizzes over the years. I went straight through from my undergraduate degree in psychology to earning my master's and doctorate degrees in clinical psychology. It just happened to work out that way because I was not yet married and didn't have any children yet. Looking back, I can appreciate completing the bulk of my education while I was still single, because there sure was a lot less to juggle back then!

I became a clinical psychologist at the age of 27, and I quickly found out that in working with children, the fact that I was young and not yet a parent seemed to many of my clients to be a "liability", rather than an "asset". When new clients were scheduled with me, it was not uncommon for them to tell me, "You look too young to be a doctor". This was frequently followed up by the question, "Do you have any children?" and I could see in their eyes that they questioned my ability to help their family when my answer was, "No." One day, a new client remarked to me that I was "quite young to be a doctor". Expecting this remark to be negative (as it always had been in the past), I braced myself to hear yet another person doubt my skills as a psychologist. I was pleasantly surprised, however, when this client followed up her statement by saying, "I think it's great that you're young and you're a doctor. You have a lot of time to help people." I don't think she knew what a gift she gave me that day, and how much I appreciated that comment that eternally reframed the negative self-perspective I had about my age.

I don't have any problems these days being seen as too young to be a doctor. In fact, I remember joking with a client just the other day that my credibility as a psychologist increased once I had children of my own. Now when I am asked whether I have any children, I can say, "I have three young adult sons", and the response that I receive back is often one of surprise and awe!

I received my undergraduate degree in psychology from Xavier University in Cincinnati. I was what you might call the stereotypical college student, in that I lived in the dorms (later in an apartment with 3 other girls) and highly enjoyed my college experience. After receiving my undergraduate degree, I proceeded directly on to Indiana University of Pennsylvania in western Pennsylvania and enrolled in the doctoral program in clinical psychology, where I received both my master's and my doctorate degree. I was one of the youngest students in my class—many of my classmates had more life experience than I and had worked for some years prior to beginning their doctorate program. Several of my classmates were older and had spouses or children; some of them faced the challenges of being single parents while attending school full-time. They used to tell me that juggling school while having a family was both an added stress as well as an additional blessing; they had to be concerned with needs other than their own, but they also had many fun diversions from their life as a student. This was in direct contrast to my own experience, where although I only had to focus on taking care of one person--myself, the downside was that I also did not live with a family of my own whom I could turn to in difficult times.

The challenge that I am aware of now for other moms who are currently students is to find a balance between being successful in school and managing the other areas of their lives well. I thought it might be helpful to share some ideas that other students who are also mothers and wives have found helpful to them, in the hopes that you might benefit from trying some of these tips yourself.

One of the difficult parts about being a student while having children of your own is being able to find ways to get your studies and assignments done amid a busy family life. Some women find it helpful to do the bulk of their schoolwork away from home—at the library, the coffee shop, or some other quiet place. This helps them to better compartmentalize the "student" role from the roles of "mother" and "wife". There are far less distractions at the library than there are at home. You will not be staring at dirty dishes, dusty furniture, or laundry that needs to be washed when you are surrounded by books and quiet tables of studious peers. In addition, you will not have to multi-task and try to meet the needs of your children while you are poring over copious notes about economics or studying the anatomy of the nervous system.

Other moms find creative ways to study at home instead. Moms with school-aged children might find that they can be productive when they arrange the bulk of their studying to be done during the school day, while their kids are not at home. For moms who have younger children who are not yet in school full-time, hiring a babysitter or a "mother's helper" to help watch their kids while studying in a different part of the house can be helpful. Sometimes students in the homeschool community are available to help entertain your kids during the day.

When you are both a mother and a student, it is essential that you try to plan ahead for ways to streamline your life and your workload at home. It is a set-up for failure for you to expect "Superwoman" accomplishments of yourself at any time, but especially when you have an additional role that requires extra time and energy. One thing that will be invaluable is for you to prioritize those things that are most important to you and give yourself permission to let the other things slide.

Exercise 7—Evaluating the Importance of Other Areas of your Life While Keeping your Student Role a Priority

Step One: Look at the following list and rank order each of these areas from 1 to 10 based upon their level of importance to you. The area of most importance to you would be labeled "1" and the area of least importance to you personally would be labeled "10". Keep in mind that the way in which you rank these areas is a personal decision—there is no "right" or "wrong" way to rank them. Just rank them according to what feels right to you.

_____ A tidy house (little to no clutter)

_____ A clean house (little to no dirt)

_____ Home-cooked meals for your family (as opposed to "fast food")

_____ Quality time with your kids (uninterrupted/ undivided attention)

_____ Being present at your children's activities (e.g. sports games, school conferences, dance recitals)

_____ Regular connection with your spouse

_____ Managing a tight budget (finding economical ways for recreation, shopping, eating)

_____ "Down" time for you (physical exercise, socializing with "the girls")

_____ Being engaged with your children's homework

_____ Other: (list anything else that might be important to you but is not yet listed)

Step Two: Once you have rank-ordered these areas of your life in terms of their importance to you, transfer each of the areas to the number below that corresponds with your ranking of that area. For example, if you ranked "Being present at your children's activities" as Number One, write that down next to the number 1 listed below. (Ignore the "M/O/combo" for now.)

1. M/O/combo _____
2. M/O/combo _____
3. M/O/combo _____
4. M/O/combo _____
5. M/O/combo _____
6. M/O/combo _____
7. M/O/combo _____
8. M/O/combo _____
9. M/O/combo _____
10. M/O/combo _____

Step Three: Your next task is to decide which areas you want and/or need to do yourself, and which areas you would be okay with enlisting others to help. Go back to the list above and circle "M" (mom) for those areas you want/need to do yourself, circle "O" (others) for those areas which you are okay with letting others help you out, and circle "combo" (combination) for those areas that you want to be involved in but can also use other people's help with.

In deciding whether to circle "mom", "others" or "combo", keep in mind how big a role both time and money currently play in your family's current cycle of life. In certain seasons of our lives, time is a more precious commodity, and we are willing to pay a little extra in order to have that extra time that we need. In other seasons of our lives, our family's budgets are tighter, and we need to be more conscious of our money, which might mean doing more things on our own or creatively swapping tasks with other people.

For example, if a clean house is of high importance to you and your budget allows it, you might choose to hire someone to clean your house on a weekly, biweekly, or monthly basis. This frees up your time from household chores and allows you to dedicate that time to other areas of your life. When I was working outside of the home part-time and caring for three young boys ages 3 and under, my mother-in-law convinced my husband that hiring someone to come in to clean our house would greatly reduce my stress level and enable us to run our home more smoothly. (My own mother died when I was 19, so it was truly a blessing to have such a caring mother-in-law in my life!) Although we lost her to COVID, my mother-in-law always seemed to support me and was frequently able to convince my husband of things that I needed, particularly if I had problems convincing him of those things myself! The cleaning service is a perfect example of this. When I first brough up the idea to my husband, he was a little reluctant to embrace it, but his mom spoke from the wisdom of having raised two small boys close in age while working full-time as a teacher, and this helped him to eventually concede (Thanks, Nana!).

However, if a clean house is important to you and your budget is tighter, perhaps you can come up with a solution for enabling the help of your friends in this area. A group of four moms that I knew years ago had a creative arrangement that worked for them. Each week, three of them would descend upon one of the moms' homes and spend two or three hours cleaning it from top to bottom, while the fourth mom whose house it was, would watch all the other moms' children during this time at one of their homes. This way, each mom received a very thorough housecleaning once a month, which made it so much easier for her to maintain it the rest of the time.

The next chapter will offer an even greater variety of ideas and ways to streamline household tasks. However, the purpose of listing this particular exercise in the chapter about being a student is to help you start to think about how to structure your life so that you can fit the role of "student" into the other responsibilities that you already have. Sometimes we forget that when we are enrolled in classes, we are adding student responsibilities on top of an already-full stack of plates in our lives. Without consciously planning how to manage this additional role effectively, we most certainly will feel burned out, stressed out, tired, and depressed.

A common feeling that all people experience at times when they are students is panic. Maybe you are panicking now just from hearing the word! Many times, panic goes hand in hand with procrastination. When the deadline for a big project that we are assigned looms ahead in the near future, and we have very little done for it yet—panic is inevitable! The good news is that panic resulting from procrastination is avoidable if we simply buckle down and do the work that we need to do.

An article published years ago in Psychology Today addressed the subject of procrastination by suggesting that one major reason most people procrastinate is that we have problems with "deferring gratification." In simple layperson's terms, this means that people often procrastinate because they do what they want to do rather than do what they need to do. Very often, what we need to do is research articles for that paper or read more chapters in that book, but what we want to do is binge-watch our favorite Netflix episodes of Bridgerton or look through the latest issue of People and catch up on the celebrity gossip. It requires self-discipline to put off our desires and focus instead on the work that needs to be done, when our desires are so much more instantly rewarding (i.e. gratifying) and entertaining. To be successful students, we need to become better at "deferring gratification" and condition ourselves to receive those rewards after we have completed our work, and not before.

How many children would eat all their vegetables if they were allowed to have dessert first? In fact, we teach our kids, "Eat your peas, and then you may have a cookie." How do you think it would go if we passed out the cookies first and then placed a pile of peas on their plates afterwards?? In the same way, if you get in the habit of "deferring gratification" by pushing yourself to work on your schoolwork first, and then afterwards allow yourself the reward of indulging yourself in some way, you will likely find much more success. When I felt forced to read a particularly boring chapter in graduate school, sometimes I would reward myself with one M&M after each page that I finished. Other times, I would set a goal of a time frame for working on my schoolwork or requiring that I complete a particular assignment, and then allow myself the privilege of going to the park or watching a T.V. show. By following the simple logic of letting the reward follow the required tasks, I was much more successful in getting the job done.

Another way to tackle procrastination is to avoid the trap of perfectionism. If you tend to be a perfectionist by nature (as I am, and which I learned goes hand-in-hand with being a Virgo!), you may often procrastinate because you want the end result to be perfect. What I like to try to remember is that in writing a paper, for instance, it is much easier to just get started writing, (no matter how "rough" the rough draft of it is), because I am aware that editing something that is already written is always easier than writing a perfect paper from start to finish. Sometimes the "anticipatory anxiety" we feel in thinking about a task is far worse than the actual task itself. How many times have you dreaded doing something, only to find out once you forced yourself to do it, that "it wasn't so bad after all!"? By breaking down longer-term assignments into more bite-sized, shorter assignments, you may find yourself more equipped to tackle daunting school tasks. When we were in elementary, middle-school, and sometimes even high school, our teachers often helped us to tackle longer projects by requiring small parts of the project to be handed in before the finished product was due. For instance, they required us to follow the steps of:

a. choosing a topic and submitting it for approval,

b. preparing an outline of the paper,

c. turning in a rough draft of the paper,

d. making corrections and then turning in a second draft, and then

e. submitting the final project.

By breaking a big project into smaller chunks with earlier due dates, we were able to successfully complete the assignment. Even though nobody is requiring you to follow this procedure now, it can be invaluable for you to adopt this same format whenever you are assigned a big paper or a long-term project. Take the final product and break it down into smaller tasks, then give yourself earlier deadlines to complete each part. You may be surprised at what you can accomplish this way!

In Chapter Six, which focused on Plate 3: Excelling at Work, I mentioned that I try to follow the helpful tip of: "Study for 45; break for 15." I explained that this meant that I spend 45 consecutive minutes totally focused on my reading (or writing or researching) and then take a break for the next 15 minutes (to get a snack, to check my e-mail, to return a phone call). This way, I don't get distracted by numerous, little interruptions throughout my entire study time. If I think of something that I need to be doing other than my studies, rather then getting up during that focused 45-minute time frame, I write it down and then get up and do it during my 15-minute break. I can't take credit for coming up with this idea, however. I gleaned it from reading a research summary of the habits of effective C.E.O.'s of Fortune 500 companies. The research considered the length of time that our brain can remain focused on a task. The average length of time that a typical person can focus on a task without his or her attention wandering was found to be no longer than 45 minutes. That said, it will be much more productive for you to spend three 45-minute chunks of time focused on work, interspersed with three 15-minute breaks after each one, than it would be for you to spend three solid hours working on an assignment. This is how I studied during my graduate school training, how I got through a mound of paperwork at my office, and how I wrote the bulk of this book.

Another idea for students can be especially helpful when you find yourself faced with completing a time-intensive project, long paper, thesis, or dissertation. This idea was suggested by my dad, who earned his master's degree in mathematics, completed almost all of his work towards his Ph.D., and had a long, successful career as a math and computer teacher. (He also knew a thing or two about being a successful student!) He suggested this to me when I was struggling to complete my doctoral dissertation. At that time, I had great difficulty disciplining myself to sit down and write for long periods of time, day after day after day. His suggestion was that when I finish my work for that day, I then make a note on where I needed to start the next time I sat down to write. Basically, he said that by taking a few minutes at the end of each writing session to make a note on what I needed to accomplish at the next writing session, I would save myself a lot of time because I would no longer have to ask myself, "What should I do now?" the next day when I returned to my writing. This was an extremely valuable tip for me, and one that I continue even as I wrote this book today.

One important thing to remember is that you will always be a mother, but you are only a student for a temporary part of your life. This "temporary" time may feel never-ending (especially if you are a part-time student or have many years of education ahead of you for the career that you desire), but it will in fact end at some future point. It may take one year; it may take several years; but it will not last forever. Your role as a student is an investment in your future, and it is a means to an end. At the end of this journey lies a better job, additional income, a more satisfying career, exciting opportunities, and new skills and training.

It may be encouraging to you to post visual reminders that help you remember to keep the end of your role in mind. When I was in graduate school (for what did, in fact, seem like FOREVER!), there were many times that I wrote out, "Dr. Sharon Janowiak" (my maiden name) to myself so that I could visualize what that title would look like at the end of this very long journey. Without these visual reminders, it can be so easy (as the cliché goes) "to not see the forest because of the trees". It is important to keep the big picture in mind.

Think of ways to involve your children in your responsibilities as a student. Can they help make flash cards for you? Can they quiz you on test material? Can they sit next to you and read their books while you do your own reading as well? Can they help decorate your study area with encouraging drawings, posters, or signs? Imagine how motivating it would feel to look up from your computer and glance at a picture made by your child that said, "You can do it, Mom! I believe in you!" Children love to contribute, and if you help them find ways to involve them in your life as a student, they will be less resentful about the time you need to spend away from them and feel more empowered that they can be a help to you.

Chapter 8

Plate 5: Keeping Your Household Running Smoothly

Many years ago, I heard a pastor preach a sermon on "The Burden of the Blessing". He spoke about how the blessings we receive also come with burdens—the money we earn comes with taxes to pay, bigger families come with more mouths to feed, a more spacious home comes with more rooms to clean. This was a lightbulb moment for me that much of what we grumble about is really "the burden of the blessing"!

I came across a poem that I adapted for myself in an abbreviated form several years ago. It served as a reminder of how our household chores are in actuality the burdens of our blessings. Here is the original version of the poem:

Lord, thank you for this sink full of
dirty dishes; we have plenty to eat.

*Thank you for this pile of dirty laundry, for it
reminds me we have lots of nice clothes to wear.*

*And I would like to thank you, Lord, for those
unmade beds; they were so warm and comfortable
last night. I know that many have no bed.*

*My thanks to you, Lord, for this bathroom,
complete with all the splattered mirrors, soggy,
grimy towels and dirty lavatory; they are so convenient.*

*Thank you for this finger-smudged refrigerator that needs
defrosting so badly; it has served us faithfully for many years.
It is full of cold drinks and enough leftovers for two or three
meals.*

*Thank you, Lord, for this oven that absolutely must be
cleaned today. It has baked so many things over the years.*

*The whole family is grateful for that tall grass that needs
mowing, the lawn that needs raking; we all enjoy the yard.*

*Thank you, Lord, even for that slamming door.
My kids are healthy and able to run and play.*

*Lord, the presence of all these chores awaiting me
says you have richly blessed my family. I shall do
them cheerfully and I shall do them gratefully.*

Author Unknown.

I invite you to create your own version of this poem,
so that it feels like a personal prayer to you. Additional

things you might include are: pet hair that reminds us of the creatures that provide us with unconditional love and affection, our grocery list that reflects the abundance of food that is available at our fingertips, and our cars that have to be washed and maintained, which remind us of the privilege of getting from place to place quickly and safely without waiting in the sun or the cold for a bus.

In our home, we have a saying: "First world problems!" We use this to remind each other in our family that most of the things that irritate and annoy us are minor inconveniences that mean so little in the grand scheme of things. For example, in our world today, there are 2.2 billion people who live without access to safe drinking water (www.water.org). Having visited the Philippines several times in my life and having seen the extent of poverty in some parts of that country, I never want to forget the struggle some people have just to survive. Keeping all that in mind, I do want to share a little bit of what has helped me when it comes to keeping our household running smoothly.

Housework

First, let's talk about housework. Being a Type A personality and a perfectionist by nature, it took me a while to embrace that truth that when it comes to housework, there is no shame if you need help. As I mentioned in the last chapter, when my boys were little, one of the best gifts I received from my mother-in-law was the services of a weekly cleaning lady, so that the rest of the week I could just focus on maintaining the house. I remember being in my own therapy session years ago and sharing with my therapist my struggle to take care of three little kids, work part-time, and keep my house clean. My therapist responded by informing me that there were many women who stayed at home full-time and still hired people to help clean, and that it was not a reflection of poor character if I needed to enlist some outside help. It was a new idea for me.

An important thing to remember is that the younger the child, the more he or she wants to help, but the less they are actually 'helping' you. Their efforts to sweep, for example, might lead to more dirt on the floor than in the dustpan. While it would certainly be more time-efficient and effective in the short-term to do all the housework yourself, it is invaluable to give your toddler or preschooler child-sized versions of your cleaning tools (e.g. vacuum cleaner, broom and dustpan) while they are still interested, even if you have to clean after they "clean" an area. This way, when they are older and more "helpful", they will already have the desire to do chores around the house. Otherwise, you will have "shooed them away" when they are young and want to copy you, and then when they are bigger they will no longer want to help you out!

You may find it useful to consider creating "chore charts" with incentives for kids for helping around the house. When I was young, my dad created a spreadsheet on the computer (mind you, this was in the 1970's!) with the names of me and my two brothers, and 3-4 chores listed by each of our names that had to be done by Sunday night. Since my parents wanted to make sure they didn't discriminate between us by gender, the chores were rotated each week equally: I had to cut the grass just as my brothers had to clean the bathrooms and the kitchen floor. (The irony was that we kids drifted towards certain chores anyway and were allowed to "trade" chores with one another—I preferred the detail-oriented bathroom cleaning and in return I gladly traded the heat and the bugs for someone else to take over cutting the grass!)

There are age-appropriate chores for every age and stage—even toddlers can help put their own toys away! Here are some examples of age-appropriate chores:

Ages 2-3	Put toys away, clean up spills, put books away, water plants
Ages 4-5	Make bed, help load dishwasher, bring in mail, feed pet, put dirty clothes in laundry basket, help put away groceries
Age 6-8	Help sweep/vacuum, empty dishwasher, fold laundry, walk pet, prepare breakfast, help prepare dinner, set table
Ages 9-11	Do laundry, wipe down bathroom, clean mirrors, mop/scrub floors, take garbage out
Ages 12+	Plan and prepare family meals, clean bathrooms, iron, wash car, clean out fridge, wash windows

When it comes to housework, remember there is a distinction between "deep" cleaning and "maintenance" cleaning. Depending on your available time/preference/ feasibility, you can arrange your own time frame for deep cleaning vs. maintenance cleaning. I know families who do their deep cleaning once a week, every two weeks, or once a month. Sometimes a house cleaning service is hired to do the deep cleaning, while the rest of the family keeps the house in order and maintains the neatness until the next deep clean. One tip is to keep regular cleaning supplies in every area to make it easier to keep things tidy (e.g. in each bathroom keep a separate bottle of window cleaner, counter wipes, and bleach cleaner spray so that the room can be given a quick once over on a daily or every other day basis).

There are a lot of things to remember in keeping a house in order. On a Martha Stewart show, I once learned how Martha used her calendar to take the guesswork out of "When did I do _ ___ last?" She used her calendar to keep track of the dates for changing A/C filters, replenishing salt in water softeners, etc. There are likely some newer apps that can do the same thing using your smartphone, and it's a concept worth noting.

Not all of us have a natural gift for housecleaning. If this is you, I encourage you to talk to your girlfriends about how they tackle jobs—some of us are naturally skilled at cooking, others at cleaning, others at organizing— you don't need to re-invent the wheel! I learned from one neighbor that she had a habit of cleaning out her refrigerator the night that the garbage was taken out for the week, so that all the spoiled or unwanted food didn't lay around in the outside garbage can for a long time. Easy, but ingenious at the same time!

"What's for Dinner?"

Apparently, this question has been around for ages. My mother-in-law told me that her two boys used to ask her this all the time when they were young even when she and her sons all walked into the house at the same time after school where she and her husband were teachers and the boys were students. I guess some things never change!

One helpful idea for the dinner dilemma is to designate certain nights for different meals. For the longest time, Friday night was pizza night in our house, and we also had a regular taco night. Other ideas include chicken night, Mexican night, pasta night, leftover night, seafood night, crock pot night, casserole night, and vegetarian night. Having these "food titles" for each night helps narrow down ideas when it comes to dinner and can capitalize on favorites that your family enjoys.

Another idea is that as your children get older, you may want to consider assigning each child a certain day of the week that they can be in charge of preparing a dinner of their choosing. Not only does this relieve Mom and Dad of the pressure of getting dinner ready, but it also provides children with much-needed cooking skills and increases their interest in eating the foods that they have a hand in preparing. Many children that I worked with in my psychology practice have beamed at me proudly, as they rattled off a meal or two that they can cook at home, and which their family enjoys.

Although it might seem obvious, you'd be surprised by how many families don't keep a running grocery list on your refrigerator door so that each family member can write down things that are needed when they think of them. Quite often, the only time we think of an item is when we reach for it in the fridge or the pantry and find we are out of it! You can also use a phone app so that everybody in your family has access to the grocery list, and you can inform your family when the next grocery store run is, so that they can add to the list the items that they want.

Planning is critical when it comes to answering the question, "What's for dinner?" I found that the weeks that went the smoothest when it came to mealtime where the ones where I shopped for the week's meals in advance, and then posted a schedule on the refrigerator door. This helped me organize my grocery list, plan for quick meals on the nights when we had little time, and more involved meals on those nights when I had more time to prepare.

As I mentioned earlier, I worked a lot of afternoons and evenings based on the clients that I worked with (kids and teens). Throwing together a casserole in the morning before I started my day and writing the cooking instructions in a Sharpie on the tinfoil wrapping helped my husband (and my boys, as they got older), to have a home-cooked meal even when I wasn't there. I've tried it all—preparing double batches and putting one serving in the freezer, prepping meals together with friends and neighbors as a "girls' night", getting fresh heat-and-eat ready meals from Costco, cooking a big pot of chili or soup and preparing meals for the week ahead on Sunday.

Just as there are different seasons of a family life cycle, there will be different seasons for different ways to tackle meals. For example, basketball is the one sport in our house that all of our boys played. There was one year when each of our boys were on a different level team-- Freshman, J.V., and Varsity, and so we would spend two evenings a week from 4:00 pm – 9:00 pm in the bleachers at the high school. During this time, I often packed my dinner and brought it with me to the game, so that I wasn't forced to have a steady diet of concession stand food two nights a week. Another year, we had six basketball games and 12 different practice times each week to coordinate, so dinner was often on the run, and we didn't seem to have many meals together as a family during that time.

A word about preparing, serving, and cleaning up dinner (or any other meal, for that matter): everyone in the family eats, so make it an understanding that everyone helps out. I can't tell you the number of families I have worked with where Mom or Dad are so stressed out because their kids have never been required to help out at mealtime. Once when I gave a presentation about responsibility in kids, a parent shared that she felt that it was her job to do all the housework herself since she was a stay-at-home mom, and she didn't want to ask her kids to help out, as she wanted them to "enjoy being kids". Needless to say, I disagreed! (Tactfully, but strongly nevertheless!) When I grew up and then when I got married, we had a rule in our family that I know is common in many families: whoever cooks, doesn't clean up. Even the youngest child can set the table. When our boys were little, we placed their plastic plates, bowls, cups, and "silver"ware in a bottom cabinet drawer where they could reach for the items themselves and this helped them learn to set the table from a very early age.

Laundry

Families have different systems for this, and what works for one family may not work for another. Some families have designated "laundry days" (e.g. Saturday) when all the laundry is done at the same time. I know a family with older kids that assigns days of the week to each family member, so that each person has an opportunity to have access to the washer and dryer and each person does their own laundry. The thing to remember is that laundry is not considered "done" unless it has rotated through all its four stages of "undone"—washed, dried, folded, and put away. Laundry that remains folded and in baskets adds to clutter in one's house and quickly becomes unfolded (!), as baskets are rummaged through in search of a particular clothing item that is needed!

Take advantage of the many books that are out there that have been written by professional organizers and that offer various "systems" for keeping homes tidy and organized. You may even be interested in hiring a professional organizer of your own who can help you develop an ongoing system that works for you and your family. This can be money well spent and invested in a less-stressful future. Remember that there is no "one right system"; the system that works for you and your family is the "right" one!

Exercise Eight—Applying C.E.O. Strategies to Your Household

You may have never thought of yourself in these terms, but YOU are the chief executive officer (C.E.O.) of your family! Use the following checklist to assess your strengths and weaknesses, and create a strategic plan for your household tasks in the areas of housecleaning, meals, and laundry:

Housecleaning

T/F   A clean house is important to me.

___   Rank how important a clean house is to you.
       (rank: 1-10, 1 = low importance, 10 = high)

T/F   I look forward to cleaning.

T/F   I have a method for keeping my house clean that
       works well for me.

T/F   I often feel overwhelmed when it comes to
       cleaning my house.

T/F   I feel that the division of chores is satisfactory in
       our household.

T/F   My kids have assigned chores that they do
       in our home.

T/F   My kids could use more motivation to get their
       chores done.

T/F   My house is put back in order at the
       end of the day.

T/F   I would gladly swap housecleaning for
       other duties.

T/F   My cleaning method takes more time than I want
       to devote to it.

Meals

T/F   I am usually trying to figure out at the last
       minute what to have for dinner.

T/F   I find myself going to the grocery store more
       than twice a week.

T/F   It is important to me that my family have healthy
       meals. (rank: 1-10, 1 = low importance, 10 = high)

T/F   I enjoy cooking.

T/F   Our family has a structure for dinner meals that
       works well for us.

T/F I often feel overwhelmed when it comes to getting dinner on the table.

T/F I would like more help from family members with preparing dinner.

T/F I would like more help from family members with cleaning up after meals.

T/F My family is usually happy with what we have for dinner.

T/F I need more information on how to prepare dinners that are healthy, yet don't have me spending hours a night in the kitchen.

Laundry

T/F At this very moment, if you were to step into my house, you would find one or more baskets of clean clothes that need to be either folded or put away.

T/F I enjoy the process of doing laundry.

T/F A lot of time/stress could be saved in our family if we had more efficient ways of managing our laundry.

T/F The number of socks in our laundry room without a match are more than the number of people in our home.

T/F I often feel overwhelmed with the piles of dirty clothes in our home.

T/F Our family has a system whereby each family member pitches in to help with laundry.

T/F I want to equip my children so that they know how to do their own laundry once they live on their own.

Once you have answered each of the true/false items above, look at those statements that point to your dissatisfaction with the task. Try to evaluate each statement and brainstorm ways to improve those areas. If you find yourself stuck, consult with others that might be able to help you—a girlfriend, a neighbor, a parent, or a spouse. A lot of information can also be found on the Internet. There are several blogs, podcasts, and apps that address household management and housekeeping chores and can help streamline this part of your life.

Chapter 9

Plate 6: Connecting Through Friendships

G rowing up, I lived in a number of different states (and even on an island for four years). My family moved from Chicago to Guam when I was 10 years old. The summer before I started high school, we left Guam and moved to Louisville, Kentucky. After graduating from high school, I spent my college years in Cincinnati at Xavier University. From Xavier, I moved to western Pennsylvania where I spent four years in graduate school at Indiana University of Pennsylvania. As part of the requirement for my doctoral degree in clinical psychology, I completed a one-year pre-doctoral internship in Hartford, Connecticut. I feel incredibly blessed that I have always found other females to establish strong friendships with throughout each stage of my life. The bridesmaids in my wedding party were representative of some of these stages; they included friends from college, graduate school, and my internship year.

I feel my relationships with other women are essential to my mental health and well-being. Losing my mom when I was 19 years old and a sophomore in college made it important for me to find women who were a little older than me to help mentor me. They showed me what that next stage in life was like—whether it be getting my first "grown-up" job, being married, having children, or raising teenagers.

When I was pregnant with my first son, it was invaluable to connect via the Internet on a message board with other moms who were pregnant and who were due the same month my baby was due. We shared pregnancy stories, then later birth stories, and developmental milestones. I loved posting messages on that board because when I had insomnia, I could connect with other pregnant or new moms and felt like I was never alone in trying to decide what was "typical" or "atypical", especially throughout that first year of being a mom for the first time.

After having children of my own, I traded my Internet moms group for a "real-life" moms group and met other moms in my community. In fact, I met one of my dearest friends in a Moms Day Out program when our oldest boys were just three years old, and we've remained close friends ever since. Our initial conversations mainly centered around dealing with temper tantrums and managing potty training, while over the years our talks have transformed into themes relevant to raising young men—understanding their independence, discussing their relationships with young women, and nurturing our mother-son bonds.

Although we are great friends now, we like to laugh at how we didn't like each other when we first met; she thought I was a stuck-up "working mom" and I thought she was a fake, too-perky, entitled "stay-at-home" mom. It's funny how wrong first impressions can be!

Bible study groups with other women have always been important to me. When our children were young, several of us moms used to take turns hosting Bible studies at each other's homes, and we'd all chip in a few dollars to give to a couple of tweens or teens who would entertain our kids in another room for an hour or two while we moms delved into our discussion about how to grow our relationships with God. For several years, I was in a Bible study with some lovely women whose children were all college-aged and beyond, (and some who were even grandmothers) and we did the best we could with our busy schedules to meet every week to learn and grown in our walk with God.

Of course, lest you think that I "overspiritualize" my relationships with my girlfriends (!), let me also share that I also fondly remember being a part of a "Moms' Game Group" when my kids were young. During this season of our lives, we met in the evenings once a month and took turns rotating houses, while our husbands stayed home and put our children to bed. We moms all quickly found that alcohol and silly games combined to create a foolproof recipe of side-splitting laughter, a much-needed stress reliever from the stresses of parenting. I discovered that this was a group of women that I could totally "be myself" with, and although some of us were stay-at-home moms, while others worked part-time, or full-time, what bonded us together were the similarities (and hilarities!) of parenting.

Women also got me active in working out regularly. I took part in my first fitness adventure (I would say "competition", but that wouldn't be accurate since the course was untimed) with a group of eight other women (some of us who had not exercised regularly for some time) in a fun-filled event called the "Dirty Girls Mud Run". We donned matching pink tank tops with glitter letters that were more brown than pink at the end of the "race" (again, using that term loosely) after getting through a 5K course of obstacles like crawling on your belly through mud under a rope net and scaling over a wooden wall. (For those of you fitness aficionados out there, think of the cast of the movie "Bridesmaids" taking part in a Spartan Race!)

The neat thing about this mud run was that it got me started running--something that I had never been interested in before in my life. I ran my first "official" 5K soon after that, progressing to 10Ks, 15Ks, half-marathons, and then one single, solitary, full marathon. I did this with women (and sometimes their husbands) and we motivated each other through our training runs by talking through issues and "solving the world's problems" (as some of my friends would jokingly say). Running with my girlfriends got me out of bed at 6:00 am on Saturday mornings, sometimes in subzero weather and other times in the heat and humidity of a Cincinnati summer day.

More than 30 years after we first met, three of my college girlfriends and I continue to keep in touch, and we plan "Girls Getaway" weekends every so often. Our goal has always been to meet once a year, but with 12 children among us (including two sets of twins!), that hasn't always been possible. Truth be told, there is truly nothing like meeting up with an old friend that you haven't seen for a year or more and being able to pick right back up in conversation like you just saw each other yesterday. Those are rare friends, indeed, and relationships that I cherish.

My husband and I were blessed to have our first home be a new construction house. We were married in the living room of that home on Valentine's Day in 1997, and over the years we have been fortunate to develop great relationships with some of our neighbors, as our subdivision was all newly constructed homes. At the time we moved in, many of our neighbors either had had no children yet or had very young children. As the years went by, we created rituals of getting together that we all enjoyed: chili cook-offs, Christmas cookie exchanges, and firepit gatherings. By far the highlight of all these memories was the annual block party organized and held by our street. The block parties included movie nights in the dark in our backyard, a dunking machine, a bouncy house, a snow cone machine, the local firefighters who brought their trucks and sprayed water in the street for the kids to play in, and way too many hotdogs, hamburgers, and s'mores to count. At one point we even had a map of the street which depicted each home along with phone numbers and names of the family members living there. We had a strong sense of community that evolved as our neighborhood evolved and we enjoyed going-away parties to bid farewell to neighbors who had moved and gatherings to welcome new families in with chocolate-chip cookies. We supported one another with updates of family celebrations (new babies, graduations) and personal struggles (illnesses, surgeries, deaths in the family), and we were quick to bring over a casserole or a fruit basket to commemorate these occasions. Currently, a few of the homes on our street are now occupied by the second generations of family members who first moved in—our oldest son lives in our home, (as my husband and I moved to Florida), and the house across the street is now occupied by the son and daughter-in-law of their parents, who have moved to Tennessee. What a blessing our street has been to us over the years!

Another type of friendship that I have experienced as being incredibly valuable has been the married couples that my husband and I have forged relationships with over the years. I believe that it is an asset to your marriage to surround yourself at times with other couples who also genuinely love and care about each other. This is not necessarily an easy task. Divorce is at such a high rate these days, and even in intact marriages, there are those couples who fuss at each other and put each other down, to the point that it can feel extremely awkward to be around them. It can also be challenging to discover another married couple where you enjoy the wife's company, and the husbands get along together as well. If you and the other woman get along but your husbands do not, you may hear your spouse voice some reluctance at getting together with the other couple (as when my husband said that he didn't need me to arrange any "playdates" for him!). Yet another obstacle to overcome is to find other couples who share similar interests to you and your husband. Let's face it, we all know that some couples like to drink and party, while other couples prefer more reserved activities like bowling and card games. It can take quite a few "couple dates" to finally find another couple that you match up with in all these areas. However, when you do, you will find it is definitely worth it.

It will probably come as no surprise to you when I share that our friendships with other couples have also changed through different seasons of our family's life. Early on in our marriage when our children were very young, we volunteered at to host a small group "Forty Days of Purpose" which focused on Rick Warren's best-selling book, "The Purpose-Driven Life". During our gatherings, we had teenagers come and babysit all the children whose parents were members of this group, while we grown-ups met regularly and shared our thoughts, feelings, and prayed together. It was a time in our life that I remember fondly. Although we do not remain close friends with these couples and their children today, I believe that each of us who participated in that "Forty Days of Purpose" Bible study valued those weeks of learning and growing together. Sometimes the friendships that we form are for a season, and sometimes friendships last a lifetime. However, one thing they all have in common is that they all contributed an important part to me being the person who I am today.

Exercise 9—Do Your Friendships Meet Your Needs?

Friends meet many different needs for us. Since we were created to be connected to one another, place a checkmark beside any of the following things that you might feel you would need from a friend:

_____ Babysitting

_____ Girls' night out

_____ Bible study/prayer partner

_____ An ear to hear you out after a long day

_____ A shoulder to cry on when you are upset

_____ Workout buddy

_____ Someone to talk a walk with

_____ Help with driving one of your children somewhere

_____ Advice

Circle True or False as the following statements apply to you:

T/F I have only one person I can count on if I needed help.

T/F I wish I had more female friends.

T/F I don't know many of my neighbors by name.

T/F I don't currently have a "church home", but I wish I did.

T/F I find it hard to motivate myself to work out alone.

T/F I would like to have other moms to share life experiences with.

T/F I have never helped out at my child's school.

T/F I don't have anyone's phone number I could call if my child needed a ride at the last minute.

T/F I often feel lonely and isolated as a mom.

T/F As an adult woman, I find it hard to make new friends.

If after reading through this list you find that the majority of your answers were marked "false" that means that your needs are currently met by the friends that you presently have, and that is great news! You are already receiving one of life's gifts—the gift of friendship! Continue to intentionally nurture these relationships, and be conscious of other women in your life that might not be so fortunate to have good, solid friends. Perhaps you are the friend they are looking for!

If, however, you answered "true" to many of the statements above, you might find it valuable to make some new girlfriends! If you agree that this is a need of yours, but find it hard to think of where to meet new people, look through the list below and check off any ideas that you think might fit for you:

Places to meet friends:

_____ Church

_____ Neighborhood

_____ Sporting events of my child

_____ Parents of my child's classmates

_____ Co-workers

_____ Common interest event (e.g. cooking class, attending a book reading)

_____ Fitness center/gym

_____ Local park or playground

_____ Friend of a friend's

One of the best ways to make new friends is to reach out in small ways to other people. Whether it be volunteering at a local school or community event, striking up a conversation with another mom sitting alone at the park, or greeting the person next to you in your exercise class, remember that every friendship started with two people who didn't know each other at all. Smiling, making eye contact, and expressing kindness to others around you is a great beginning to any friendship!

Chapter 10

Plate 7: Making Time for Yourself

I'm sure most of you have heard the expression, "Put on your own oxygen mask first before helping your child." For those of you who haven't, this phrase refers to the instructions given by flight attendants on what to do in case an airplane experiences an emergency landing: oxygen masks will drop down from the ceiling directly above you, and parents should first put on their own oxygen mask before attempting to help their children with theirs. The rationale for this is that if we as parents lose consciousness as a result of not getting enough oxygen, we will be of no help to our children. We must first be sure we can breathe before we help them be able to breathe. This illustrates the need for moms to put themselves on the priority list!

In our culture, women are raised to be nurturers. Nurturing others is what makes motherhood so rewarding for so many women. When we were young girls, we played "house" and pretended to mother our doll babies; as we got older, many of us looked after our younger siblings or babysat for other families. After becoming mothers, we naturally took care of our children. We might have also found ourselves becoming responsible for the health and well-being of our own parents as well—as evidenced by many adults referred to as "the sandwich generation". In and of itself, nurturing others is a vital and necessary task. It is only when nurturing others takes place in the absence of us as moms nurturing ourselves that this becomes a problem. In the book, "When Pleasing Others is Hurting You", author Dr. Hawkins beautifully explains that we are to meet others' needs out of the abundance of having our own needs met, not at the expense of ourselves.

Walk up to any mother on the street, and you will find that she can talk to you about her experiences with "mommy guilt". There never seems to be enough time in the day to meet everyone's needs—our children's, our workplace's, our spouse's, our relatives', our pets'—and frequently when we don't have enough time to meet everyone's needs, the person we end up short-changing tends to be ourselves. We reason that if everyone else is doing okay, then it logically follows that we ourselves will be fine.

However, judging by the number of moms who feel burned out, stressed out, tired, or depressed at any given moment, I don't feel like we are doing a great job taking care of ourselves. For that matter, I don't think that we are doing a great job showing our children (and especially our daughters) how they should take care of themselves at the same time that they are taking care of other people. If we don't model self-care in ourselves, then we are indirectly creating a new generation of children who in turn will grow up to feel burned out, stressed out, tired, and depressed. Remember that old phrase, "The apple doesn't fall far from the tree?"

Many times, we as mothers cannot motivate or convince ourselves to make changes that are difficult or challenging EXCEPT when our children are negatively affected. There are mothers I've met with in my clinical practice who told me that the turning point in leaving an abusive relationship was when they noticed the negative impact it was having on their children. It was at that point that they were able to make a change. They felt that they could always cope with their own physical or emotional pain, but once they saw their children in pain, they decided in no uncertain terms that they needed to do something different. It is so important to make time to take care of yourself for your children's sake, in addition to your own sake. Obviously, you will both benefit but think about it in any way that you need to in order to put yourself as a higher priority on your "to-do list".

When I talk about making time for yourself, I am referring to doing those things that are healthy—spiritually, physically, and mentally. The first plate in this book had to do with spiritual health—staying in close relationship with God—so I will refer you back to that chapter if you would like to focus on improving your spiritual health. This chapter will focus instead on mental health and physical health.

As you probably already know, there is a strong correlation between mental health and physical health, often referred to as the mind-body connection. One of my favorite ways to explain this is the example I use frequently with clients to illustrate how symptoms develop. The equation is deceptively simple: **whenever our stressors outweigh our resources, we will develop a symptom.** Stressors can be *fixed* (something that we cannot do anything to change), such as the illness of ourselves or a family member, or *variable* (something that we can do something about), such as the number of activities we are committed to. Resources are those things which we use to cope with stress, such as physical exercise, asking others for help, or meditation. Symptoms can be physical or psychological, and include headaches, stomachaches, fatigue, anxiety, or depression.

Our bodies and minds are designed to withstand a certain amount of stress but as you are aware, they both have their limits. The purpose of any symptom is to signal to our bodies and our minds that something is awry. Without symptoms, we could easily overwork our bodies and our mind to our detriment. As an analogy, think of a person with diabetes who has numbness in her feet as a result of the disease. She would need to be sure to examine her feet on a daily basis because she could easily get a cut or an infection on her toe or on the bottom of her foot and never know it before it gets very bad. Since the symptom of pain is missing, the signal from the body to the brain never arrives and consequently, the person would not know that something very serious is wrong with her feet. In the same way, we need to pay attention to the symptoms (mental or physical) that show up in our minds and in our bodies and use them as opportunities to figure out what might be off-balance in our lives so that we can make some changes.

When trying to address a symptom that has occurred as the result of our stressors outweighing our resources, the first question we need to ask ourselves is, "Can we decrease our stressors?". Perhaps we need to "opt out" of activities that we have agreed to in order to free up our time, or maybe it would help to cut back on spending if we are trying to help our financial situation. Remember that we can only alter the stressors that are variable; the stressors that are fixed are just things that we are going to need to try to manage.

The second thing to look at would be to see if it is possible for us to increase our resources. Ironically, when we are under a great deal of stress we often stop doing those things that are helpful for us under the guise of "saving time" or because "we just don't feel like it." Resources such as working out, taking a calming walk, having coffee with a friend, or throwing a frisbee with our kids can be very helpful in decreasing our symptoms.

If it is "mommy guilt" that is holding you back from taking time for yourself, then think how much more your children will benefit having from a happy, healthy mom rather than a mom who is burned out, stressed out, tired, or depressed. When we make sure that we are taking care of ourselves, we have so much more to offer our children.

Exercise 10—Are You Taking Enough Time for Yourself?

Which of the following things have you done in the last day (D), week (W), or month (M)? Place a checkmark wherever it applies.

1. D _____ W _____ M _____ Eaten a meal by myself.
2. D _____ W _____ M _____ Exercised/worked out (including yoga, walking, intentional stretching).
3. D _____ W _____ M _____ Joined one or more girlfriends for an activity (e.g. meal, movie, cocktail, coffee, book club).
4. D _____ W _____ M _____ Sat quietly for at least 10 minutes.
5. D _____ W _____ M _____ Prayed or meditated.
6. D _____ W _____ M _____ Laughed out loud.
7. D _____ W _____ M _____ Gotten a haircut/manicure/pedicure.
8. D _____ W _____ M _____ Read a book or a magazine for pleasure.
9. D _____ W _____ M _____ Played a game of my choice on my phone, tablet, or computer.
10. D _____ W _____ M _____ Browsed in a physical or on-line store (as opposed to shopping with a list).
11. D _____ W _____ M _____ Taken a long bath.
12. D _____ W _____ M _____ Called a friend.
13. D _____ W _____ M _____ Enjoyed myself on Pinterest, Facebook, Instagram, or another Internet activity.

14. D _____ W _____ M _____ Daydreamed about something positive.
15. D _____ W _____ M _____ Taken a class about something I'm interested in (e.g. dance, music, cooking).
16. D _____ W _____ M _____ Spent time on a hobby I enjoy (e.g.playing a musical instrument, singing, dancing, cooking, quilting, crocheting, needlepoint, scrapbooking).
17. D _____ W _____ M _____ Listened to music that lifted or inspired me.
18. D _____ W _____ M _____ Other: _____
19. D _____ W _____ M _____ Other: _____
20. D _____ W _____ M _____ Other: _____

Review your answers above and look at any patterns that jump out at you. Maybe you discover (to your delight!) that you are doing a good job in this area, and that you are taking time to care of yourself. If so, pat yourself on the back and keep it up! Do you find that you have only a few items checked? Do your answers indicate that it's been a while since you've "indulged" in something just for you, that you enjoy? If so, use this exercise as a reminder to give yourself permission to set aside time (schedule it, if that helps) and nurture *you* by doing those things that bring you joy!

Chapter 11

Plate 8: Volunteering Time to Help Others

The last plate that I want to touch upon in this book is about volunteering. You might be saying to yourself right now, "I have enough plates already that I can't opt out of, why on earth would I want to opt in to another plate?", and if this is you, I totally understand. Our lives our busy! Our days our long, our commitments are many, and our hours of sleep are always too few! I just spent a chapter talking about the importance of decreasing stress and if your stress level right now is too high, you might be tempted to tune out the suggestion to volunteer. But I challenge you not to overlook it. Volunteering need not be a huge time commitment or a life-saving act. It can be as big as organizing an international mission trip for a large number of people on an annual basis, or as small as taking one hour a week to help someone else's child learn to read. The definition of "volunteer" is "freely offer to do something." I feel strongly that we can all freely offer to do something.

Let me give you a little background about myself. My mother was Filipina and my father is Caucasian (of Polish descent). My parents met when my father was in the Peace Corps in the Philippines and he tutored my mother in math. They fell in love, got married there, and then moved to Chicago where my two brothers and I were born. (Remember in the chapter on friendships that I mentioned I had lived for a few years in Guam?) During the four years that my family and I lived there, which for me was when I was in the 5th-8th grade, we took several trips to the Philippines, where the rest of my mom's family still lived. Guam was much closer to the Philippines than Chicago, and we wanted to take advantage of this opportunity. During my trips there, I vividly remember my young eyes being exposed to many things that were a stark contrast from how I lived in the United States. My Filipino relatives were relatively well-off, but I was deeply moved by the widespread poverty many others faced in the Philippines. I saw families living in small makeshift homes with tin roofs, children playing barefoot, with uncombed hair and worn clothing, and people of all ages gathering at large garbage sites—some were simply there, while others were looking for anything usable or edible. The modern conveniences that I took for granted in Chicago and in Guam did not exist in the Philippines. When I arrived back to Guam, and later when we moved to the United States, I never forgot what I experienced during my short time in the Philippines.

I know that I am not alone in this feeling. I am reminded by a client of mine who went on a mission trip to Haiti and after her return, she expressed how incredibly blessed she felt that she could lace up her $100 pair of running shoes, step out her front door, and run safely for miles. She shared how she had always taken this for granted before traveling to Haiti.

These thoughts come to me at random times. I can be standing in a long, slow-moving line at a restaurant and instead of grumbling at the poor service, I quietly marvel at the miracle of having enough money in my pocket to go out and purchase my choice of food that someone else will prepare for me. Sometimes when I'm at the grocery store, I am in awe over the rows and rows of varieties of food that are displayed and I can't help but think about people in other parts of the world who are not afforded this luxury. I feel silly complaining about feeling "put out" about going grocery shopping when many people go without food on a regular basis.

My children share this sentiment at times. I think I mentioned in an earlier chapter how we have a phrase in our house, "First world problems", that we use to remind each other that we really don't have it that hard here in the U.S. For example, when I get home and I am annoyed that one of my sons has parked in my parking spot in our driveway and I have to call them on my cell phone to ask them to move their car so I can park there, my son says to me, "First world problems". When one of my sons pulls open the refrigerator and then the pantry, and then goes into the garage where we have a second refrigerator and more pantry items, and comes back in the house complaining, "There's nothing around here to eat!", I tell him (you guessed it)—"First world problems."

Please know that my intent in sharing these thoughts with you is not to guilt you. If you were raised Catholic (like me) or just the simple fact that you are a mom yourself tells me that you have more than an adequate supply of guilt, of that I am certain! I share these thoughts with you because I want you to understand why I feel strongly about volunteering—about giving back. Not out of guilt, but out of gratitude—out of the desire to help others who are in less fortunate positions than my family and I are in.

In Rick Warren's book, "The Purpose-Driven Life", the first words in the book are: "It's not about you." He goes on to explain how to live an intentional life—driven by purpose—and reminds us that life is not centered around us. There are many children today who (probably not even intentionally so) are being raised with feelings of entitlement and who take everyday "luxuries" for granted— closets full of clothes, rooms full of toys, expensive technological gadgets. The authors of "Burn Your Goals" (Joshua Medcalf and Jamie Gilbert) remind us that: "Over 1 billion people on earth don't have access to clean drinking water. Even if you live on the streets in the United States your quality of life is still much greater than at least 2 billion people around the world. Over 3 billion people live on less than three dollars per day".

There are so many reasons to volunteer. Volunteering together as a family teaches our children, "It's not just about you" and exposes them to other people and situations that they might not otherwise get to experience. It helps our children learn empathy and compassion for other people. It helps us as busy moms "pan out" on our issues and focus on concerns other than our own, so that we don't get too narrowly focused on problems that are quite small in the grand scheme of things.

In my work as a psychologist, I often recommend that people who are struggling with depression find a volunteer opportunity in which to take part. Not only does it help give them a reason and a purpose to get out of bed for that day and focus on something outside of themselves, but the hours and the commitment necessary for volunteering can also be very short-term and time-limited, which is an ideal situation for someone who might feel good one day and very ill another day.

When looking to volunteer, think about helping with a cause that you are interested in—or better yet, that you are passionate about! It could be children, older adults, people with developmental disabilities, or individuals of another culture. It doesn't even have to be humans, it could be animals! Is there an issue that you feel strongly about? Is there an illness or a disability that has affected you or a loved one? Have you heard a story on the news that really spoke to your heart, and that you felt compelled to pray for? Any of these things can be a great place to start when you are trying to decide what you would like to volunteer for.

Volunteering can even come from a new interest. For example, I was a never a runner growing up. Although I played volleyball, basketball (for one season!) and did cheerleading, running was always something I despised. My memory of running was limited to the experience of debilitating side stitches while being forced to run laps around the gym in P.E. class in elementary and high school (who's with me?!). However, it was intriguing how many 5K run/walks I saw advertised on a regular basis, many held for the benefit of all sorts of causes. I knew if I were to do a 5K, it would take some training on my part (think: a couch to 5K program) and I didn't feel "moved" (no pun intended!) to take on a discipline like that for a very long time.

However, one day I saw a 5K that took hold of my heart and wouldn't let go. It was an announcement for an inaugural 5K on the 4th of July in honor of a six-year-old boy who died of brain cancer on July 4th. Here was something I could train for. It just so happened that this son's mom was a local psychologist—a colleague of mine whom I had never met—and she had lost her youngest child to this horrible illness. This was the first 5K in his honor, and one that continues every year to this day on the 4th of July. I am proud to say that I was a part of this community that rallied every year to raise money for pediatric brain cancer. During the years I lived in Cincinnati, it become an annual tradition for me, and it jump-started my love for running.

Volunteering can encompass an incredibly wide variety of activities. The best volunteer activity is one that matches a need with your unique gifts and abilities. Think about your skill set—what things do you enjoy and what are you good at doing? What are your areas of strength? Are you a strong leader? An excellent communicator? Good at cooking, sorting, or organizing? Do you enjoy playing music? Are you a great listener? Do you like to work with your hands? Do you enjoy paperwork and filing? Are you good with numbers? Do you love cleaning because of the built-in satisfaction you get when you transform an environment? Are you compassionate? Identifying what unique gifts and talents you have that you feel confident about using is a great first step towards finding a volunteer opportunity.

Additionally, you want to envision what type of setting and what activities you would enjoy and "freely offer to do" (remember, this is the definition of "volunteering") for others. Would you prefer working outside or working inside? Are you more comfortable in a one-to-one situation, with a larger group of people, or would you rather be behind the scenes? Do you want to be a part of a one-time volunteer activity or are you willing to be a part of something on a regular basis? Would you be happier doing the same thing over and over again or is variety in an activity more of what you desire? What time frame fits for you—are you looking for a late afternoon, early evening, or weekend shift?

Du you have young children, elementary-aged kids, teens, or young adults? Would you like to do something together as a family or are you interested in a father-child or a mother-child activity? What season of life are you in? If your children are younger, and you want to volunteer as a family, the volunteer activities that fit you best will be different than those you may want to take part in when your children are older.

Before my husband and I had children, we became involved in our local Big Brothers/Big Sisters program. We were each paired with a "little sib" that we did things with on a regular basis. Sometimes the four of us did things together, and sometimes we paired off and did Big Brothers things and Big Sisters activities apart from one another. We really enjoyed this program when we were in the "newly married/no children" season of our lives because we didn't have the responsibilities yet of being parents. As a Big Brother or Big Sister, the program asks for at least a one-year commitment to your Little. We enjoyed the year that we gave to the Big Brothers/Big Sisters program and have good memories of that time.

Once we had children (that is, three children in four years!), we were involved in a church where my husband became a minister. We were blessed with our first minivan and we felt called to use this new vehicle as a way to also bless others. My husband started a ministry he called the "Harvest Ministry", and with our pastor's blessing, instead of giving our tithes to our church home, we took the weekly amount and bought groceries with the money. We bagged up the groceries and delivered them house-to-house in an area not far from us where there were many people in need. We knocked on doors of strangers, asking if they needed prayer for anything. We prayed with them, gave them a bag of groceries, and went to the next home until all our bags were gone. In the late summer, we brought bookbags filled with school supplies for the children. Once when a church friend was moving and wanted to get rid of the furniture in her house, we hauled it by truck to this same neighborhood, gave out raffle tickets, and distributed the items one by one to each lucky winner—beds, bureaus, desks, and chairs.

We then expanded our territory to downtown Cincinnati, where we ministered to unhoused men and women by providing chips, water, and sandwiches made from peanut butter and jelly or meat and cheese. When others expressed an interest in joining the Harvest Ministry and we had more hands on deck, we approached Panera and got on their schedule to bag up their unused baked goods from that day's business and added that to the list of food that we distributed. When our kids were still little, we would drive downtown in our minivan, stop at Washington Park, and keep the van door open with the kids in their car seats, while people approached us, and we handed out food and prayed with and for them. With young children, it was a season in our life of great busyness and yet it felt so good to carve out time to meet other people's needs.

I have heard of moms and families doing all kinds of volunteer activities. A moms' group that I was a part of when my kids were little was on a rotating schedule to provide homecooked meals which they brought down to the Ronald McDonald House across the street from Children's Hospital. Others worked in soup kitchens, food pantries, and women's shelters. The tasks were many and varied and included preparing meals, serving food, sorting clothes, organizing food donations, and cleaning and tidying up the inside of buildings. Some families found these volunteer opportunities by word of mouth; others discovered them through advertisements in their neighborhood newspaper, through local newsletters, on the Internet, or on the radio. There were also activities organized by area churches and schools, such as signing up to help seniors by raking leaves, mowing grass, and performing odd jobs around their homes or spending a couple of hours once a week helping children with their homework. Libraries, zoos, hospitals, and pregnancy crisis centers are all great places with numerous volunteer opportunities. If you like to work with your hands, Habitat for Humanity is an incredible organization that utilizes volunteers to help build new homes for families in need.

Exercise 11: Finding the Perfect Match:

Pairing Your Strengths and Your Gifts with Volunteer Activities

Step 1: Identify A Cause.

Find an area worth volunteering for. What do you feel strongly about? Check off any ideas that appeal to you:

_____ A specific illness or disorder (e.g. cancer, ALS, Parkinson's disease, heart disease, diabetes, mental illness, Alzheimer's disease, arthritis).

_____ A particular organization (e.g. Big Brothers/Big Sisters, Children's Hospital, Red Cross, Unicef, The Salvation Army).

_____ A social issue (e.g. homelessness, hunger, poverty, illiteracy, environmental conservation, education).

_____ A certain population (e.g. women, children, animals).

Step 2: Evaluate Your Skillset.

Which of the following gifts/talents/abilities apply to you?

_____ Cleaning skills (e.g., floors, clothes, walls).

_____ Communication skills (e.g. answering the phone, public speaking, getting your ideas across).

_____ Cooking skills.

_____ Empathy (e.g. listening without judgment, sympathizing with another's situation, understanding how others feel).

_____ Interpersonal (e.g. getting along well with others, meeting new people, greeting others, making others feel good).

_____ Mentoring (guiding another individual on a 1:1 basis).

_____ Organizing (e.g. sorting, categorizing, creating charts/tables of information).

_____ Teaching (breaking down concepts so that others understand).

_____ Using Technology (e.g. computer literacy).

_____ Technical (e.g. fixing things, working with tools, appliances, wood, or machinery).

What type of environment would you prefer to work in?

_____ I prefer to work inside.

_____ I prefer to work outside.

_____ I would be happy working either inside or outside.

Step 3: Know Which Season of Life You Are In.
Recognize which stage of life your family is currently in. Check any/all of the following that apply to you and your family:

I am the mother of a:

_____ Baby/Toddler (ages birth-2)

_____ Preschool-age child (ages 3-5)

_____ School-age child (ages 6-12)

_____ Teenager (ages 13-17)

_____ Young adult (ages 18-25)

_____ Adult (26 and older)

_____ I am a grandparent (of grandchildren of any age).

Step 4: Choose The Frequency With Which You'd Like To Volunteer. (Check all that apply.):

_____ More than once a week.

_____ Weekly.

_____ Twice a month.

_____ Monthly.

_____ Quarterly.

_____ Yearly.

For how many hours at a time?

_____ 1

_____ 2

_____ 3

_____ Half-day (4-5 hours)

_____ Full-day (6-8 hours)

What part of the week?

_____ During the week (Mondays through Fridays).

_____ On the weekend (Saturday and/or Sunday).

During what time of day?

_____ Early morning (before noon).

_____ Early to mid-afternoon (12:00 pm -3:00 pm).

_____ Late afternoon/early evening (4:00 pm – 6:00 pm).

_____ Evening (7:00 pm – 9:00 pm).

Step 5: Who Would You Like To Be Included In Your Volunteer Time? (Feel free to check any/all combinations that appeal to you from the list below.):

_____ Just me.

_____ Me and my significant other (husband, fiancé, boyfriend).

_____ Me with some of my family.

_____ Me with all of my family.

Chapter 12

A Final Word

In attempting to apply the principles of the eight plates identified in this book, I do have a final word of caution: Do not get caught in the trap of trying to get your plates to spin perfectly. There will be times that all your plates come crashing down at once; for example, when you experience an unexpected loss, a life crisis, or a journey of grief. There will also be times when one of your plates falls and breaks because you chose a different one to focus on at that time and you failed to notice the plate that was quietly and methodically slowing down. **DO NOT BE DISCOURAGED!** This is not called failure; it's called life. When this happens (and I am purposely using the word "when" and not "if"), make sure to **"make space for grace"**; meaning, assess the damage, evaluate what happened, why and how it happened (e.g. due to neglect, life circumstances, etc.) and then create a **plan for repair.**

Making Space for Grace

"Making space for grace" means two things:

1. Taking responsibility and ownership for that which is yours to take, **AND**

2. Letting go and forgiving yourself, after you've assessed, evaluated, and made a plan for repair.

When "making space for grace", be intentional about balancing the line between two traps: condemnation and pride. Very often, this line can be very thin.

Condemnation is present when we beat ourselves up and believe that we are the sole cause of one of our plates to come crashing down. Condemnation is the result of viewing this as being 100% our fault, and thinking that we must be terrible people for allowing this plate to break. Common statements that people make when they have fallen prey to the trap of condemnation include:

*   "I'm a failure."

*   "I should have..."

*   "I can never do anything right."

*   "I'm a horrible person because I let this happen."

Condemnation can also be called "destructive guilt". Destructive guilt is present when we take over-responsibility for something bad happening and end up giving ourselves a life sentence of being imprisoned in that guilt without any chance for parole.

On the other end of the continuum lies the trap of pride. Pride covers up any self-responsibility that there might be for the unfortunate outcome of a plate shattering. Pride causes us to blame other people and external factors for a mistake or a problem that we were at least partial responsibility for. Common statements that people make when they have fallen prey to the trap of pride include:

- "This is all so-and-so's fault. If he/she hadn't..... then this never would have happened."

- "It wasn't my fault."

- "At least I'm still better off than so-and-so".

The way to walk between condemnation and pride is to follow the middle path of conviction. Conviction involves taking healthy responsibility for any errors we may have honestly committed that led our plate to crash, and then forgiving ourselves and realizing that we are all imperfect humans, and that each one of us makes mistakes at times. Conviction is also known as "constructive guilt". (Think: *"constructive criticism"* where the intent in delivering it is to help other people better themselves, not to make them feel bad or to punish them.) Conviction leads us to assess, evaluate, and then make a plan for repair.

Exercise 12: Assessing and Evaluating What Went Wrong

I.   Identify which plate(s) broke:

_____ Religion/Spiritual
_____ Family (Spouse/Children)
_____ Work
_____ School
_____ Household Tasks

_____ Social Life

_____ Time for Self

_____ Volunteering

II. Consider what factors might have contributed to this (check all that apply):

_____ I was focusing on another plate and overlooked this one.

_____ Life got interrupted with a crisis.

_____ I didn't spend enough time on it.

_____ I stopped caring about it.

_____ I felt overwhelmed and so I gave up.

_____ It wasn't high enough on my priority list.

_____ I didn't know it needed that much attention to stay spinning.

_____ I didn't know how to keep it spinning.

III. How often does this plate break?

_____ This is the first time.

_____ It is a rare occurrence.

_____ It happens just about every month.

_____ It breaks at least once a week.

_____ It's never fixed!

Creating a Plan for Repair

But first, the good news! Bet you didn't think that would be what I would say next, did you? It's not often that we think of the positive when we are getting ready to fix something. However, in the situation of broken plates, I think we are in dire need of an encouraging word.

The encouraging word is "kintsugi". Kintsugi comes from two words: "kin" (golden) and "tsugi" (repair). Kintsugi is the Japanese art of repairing broken pottery by mending the broken pieces with gold and then putting the whole thing back together again. The result is a piece of art that is stronger and more beautiful than the original piece. It's encouraging to know that a broken and shattered plate can be made stronger and more beautiful for the breaking when repaired with gold.

The plan you develop for repairing with gold will be individual for each person and will depend upon the answers from the assessment and evaluation questionnaire that you completed earlier. Here are those answers again, and some suggested ways to repair with gold.

_____ *I was focusing on another plate and overlooked this one.*

Kintsugi idea: Come up with a way to regularly check in on how your plates are spinning. This might be on a weekly or monthly basis, where you schedule in some time to review your plates and evaluate how things are going on each one. Decide which ones you want to spend more time on, and which ones you can devote less time to. (You may find it helpful to refer back to two important items in Chapter Two--Figure 1 which is an illustration of the eight plates and Exercise 2--Evaluating Your Plates.)

_____ *Life got interrupted with a crisis.*

Kintsugi idea: Remember that life is made up of hills and valleys, ups and downs. When a crisis hits, one's basic human needs are the first things that should be attended to; other things must necessarily be moved to the back burner. Don't be too hard on yourself for plates breaking when your life is hit with a crisis. Emotional earthquakes happen. Your power (i.e., your energy) might be out for a time. Things in your life might be shifted and/or displaced. It often takes a while for things to settle back down, and even then it is likely that life will not go back to the same exact way it was. A new normal may need to be developed. Be gentle with yourself and consider taking everything off a few of your plates except for the bare necessities. Perhaps you need to give yourself permission to let your house get a bit dirtier than you're used to it being and focus instead on making sure your family has clean clothes to wear and that there is food in the pantry. This might be the time you withdraw from any extracurricular activities that aren't absolutely necessary, like the birthday committee at work or the room mother responsibilities of your child's classroom.

_____ *I stopped caring about it.*

Kintsugi idea: Check in with yourself to see if there may also be other things that you stopped caring about.

- Are you feeling unmotivated about things on which you know you need to take action?

- Do you find yourself sleeping more, drinking alcohol more, avoiding the tasks of life?

- Has it been a while since you genuinely laughed?

These may be symptoms of depression and you can benefit from a mental health evaluation to see if there is a larger problem going on for you. If it's just that one broken plate that you stopped caring about, maybe you can put that plate away in the metaphorical cupboard for now because you don't currently have use for it. You can take it out later if you find you miss it or need it.

_____ *I felt overwhelmed and so I gave up.*

Kintsugi idea: You may benefit from going back to Chapter 10 and looking again at the psychological equation that when your stressors outweigh your resources, you will develop a symptom.

- Are you feeling stressed?

- Are there stressors in your life currently that you can eliminate?

- In turn, are there resources available that you can add to your life to make things a little easier right now for you?

Perhaps you, like many moms, have fallen into the trap of perfectionism without even knowing it. Facebook, Instagram, and other social media sites show us "the best" of others, and if we're not careful we might fool ourselves into thinking that "the best" of others is how people live 24/7. In reality, it's often just the best picture from a whole roll of film (for those of you pre-digital-age moms who remember "film"!). Make sure that what you are comparing yourself to is your best version of yourself, not the Instagram filter or the Photoshopped image. True perfection is always curated.

_____ *It wasn't high enough on my priority list.*

Kintsugi idea: Ask yourself if you're okay with it being a lower priority right now. Different seasons of our life call for different priorities. What was important to you before may not be what's important to you today, and that's perfectly okay. If you want it to be a higher priority, than make it a point to carve out time to address the needs from that plate. Schedule your regular gym workouts on your calendar like you do your other appointments if exercise is the thing you're trying to do or swap babysitting with another couple if date night is the thing you're missing out on.

_____ I didn't spend enough time on it.

Kintsugi idea: See if the time you estimated that you needed to achieve your goal was realistic or not. Sometimes we underestimate the amount of time that it takes to keep a particular plate spinning. When I lived 10 minutes away from work, it was easy for me to find myself late to work or to an appointment if I didn't remember to leave time for the commute. Seriously! I would say in my brain, "I'll be done by 3:00 pm, and then I'll get to the school by 3:00 pm", thinking I was some sort of time traveler or that I would be instantly beamed through a portal and no time would have passed. Crazy-making. On the other hand, if there are small tasks that I am avoiding or procrastinating, it has helped me in the past to actually "time" myself on how long it takes me to actually complete that particular task. For instance, did you know that I can make my bed in 3 minutes? Or that I can stack the dishwasher in only 7? It's common to overestimate the time it takes to do tasks that we dislike, which can lead to procrastination.

_____ *I didn't know it needed that much attention to stay spinning.*

_____ *I didn't know how to keep it spinning.*

Kintsugi idea: Talking to other moms who are good at that particular plate and asking them for their tips and tricks on how they keep that plate spinning so well can be very helpful. We are all blessed with different gifts and what might come naturally to one person can be the next person's biggest challenge. When my kids were little, there was a mom in my neighborhood who always had the most immaculate house. My house was not horribly messy, but it definitely wasn't winning any awards in House Beautiful magazine. She told me some ways that she kept her house clean that had never even occurred to me, and these were invaluable once I applied them myself.

I hope this book has been helpful to you in some small way, by identifying those places where you are struggling in life, and taking into account the particular season you find your family in right now. As moms, we have more similarities than differences and by sharing with one another, we can come up with an infinite number of ideas of how to help one another "spin into control". In the words of George Eliot, "What do we live for if not to make the world less difficult for each other?" Let's keep on spinning into control!

Selected Bibliography

Chapman, G. (2009). *The Five Love Languages*
Moody Publishers.

Dalton-Smith, Dr. Saundra. (2017). *Sacred Rest.*
Hachette UK.

High Conflict Institute. (n.d.). Retrieved July 9, 2024, from
https://highconflictinstitute.com/

Hawkins, D. (2010). *When Pleasing Others Is Hurting You*
Harvest House Publishers.

Kendra, A. (2021). *The Lazy Genius Way: Embrace What
Matters, Ditch What Doesn't, And Get Stuff Done.*
Waterbrook Press (A Divis.).

Klug, R. (2002). *How To Keep A Spiritual Journal: A Guide
To Journal Keeping For Inner Growth And Personal
Discovery.* Augsburg.

Lucado, M., & Bishop, J. L. (2017). *Anxious For Nothing:
Finding Calm In A Chaotic World; Study Guide Five
Sessions.* Thomas Nelson.

Medcalf, J., & Gilbert, J. (2015). *Burn Your Goals: The
Counter-Cultural Approach To Achieving Your
Greatest Potential.* Lulu Publishing Services.

Moore, B. (2017). *The Quest - Study Journal.* Lifeway
Church Resources.

Omartian, S. (2022). *The Power Of A Praying® Husband.*
Harvest House Publishers.

Ramsland, M. (2017). *Simplify Your Life Collection.*
Thomas Nelson.

Shirer, P. (2012). *Discerning The Voice Of God: How To Recognize When God Is Speaking.* Moody Publishers.

Warren, R. (2013). The Purpose Driven Life: *What On Earth Am I Here For?* Zondervan.

Weaver, J. (2007). *Having A Mary Heart In A Martha World: Finding Intimacy With God In The Busyness Of Life.* Waterbrook Press.

www.ingramcontent.com/pod-product-compliance
Lightning Source LLC
Chambersburg PA
CBHW071511290125
21070CB00032B/476